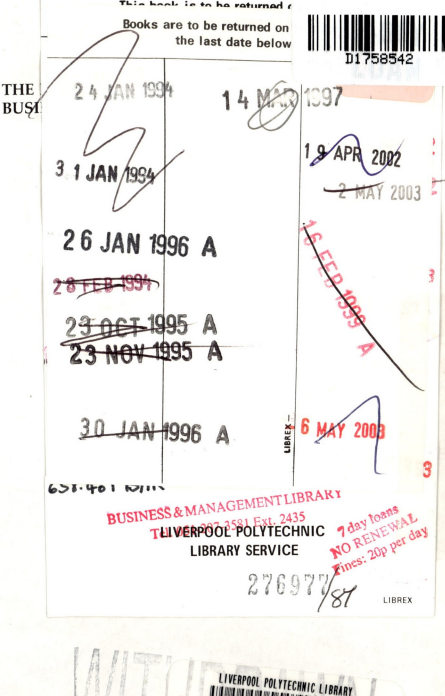

This book is to be returned

Books are to be returned on
the last date below

D1758542

THE
BUSI

24 JAN 1994

14 MAR 1997

3 1 JAN 1994

1 9 APR 2002

2 MAY 2003

2 6 JAN 1996 A

28 FEB 1994

23 OCT 1995 A
23 NOV 1995 A

16 FEB 1999 A

30 JAN 1996 A

LIBREX —

6 MAY 2003

3

658.401 BAR

THE MANAGER'S GUIDE TO BUSINESS FORECASTING

How to understand and use
forecasts for better business results

Michael Barron and David Targett

Basil Blackwell

First published, 1985
First published in paperback 1987

Basil Blackwell Ltd
108 Cowley Road, Oxford OX4 1JF, UK

Basil Blackwell Inc.
432 Park Avenue South, Suite 1505,
New York, NY 10016, USA

British Library Cataloguing in Publication Data
Barron, Michael.
    The manager's guide to business forecasting: how to understand and use
    forecasts for better business results.
    1. Business forecasting.
    I. Title.   II. Targett, David.
    338.5'44   HB3730

    ISBN 0–631–14034–4
    ISBN 0–631–15627–5 Pbk

Library of Congress Cataloging-in-Publication Data

Barron, Michael.
    The manager's guide to business forecasting.

    Includes index.
    1. Business forecasting.   I. Targett, David.
II. Title.
HD30.27.B37 1985   658.4'0355   85–9090
ISBN 0–631–14034–4
ISBN 0–631–15627–5 Pbk

Typeset by Freeman Graphic, Tonbridge, Kent
Printed in Great Britain by The Camelot Press Ltd, Southampton

Contents

Introduction

Does your organization use business forecasts? If so, are you satisfied that you are getting value for money? Have you any means of knowing whether or not you are getting value for money? Many organizations cannot answer the last question because they do not regularly appraise and monitor their forecasting system. When they do and problems are found, it is often because the forecasting process has not been properly managed, and much less often because of technical errors.

If your organization does not use business forecasts, what holds it back? Is it because forecasting seems too complex technically? Or is it because you feel unable to communicate with the technical experts who might be able to help?

This book covers both situations. Whether you are dealing with in-company experts or external consultants, its purpose is to explain what you need to know in order to use business forecasts effectively. This includes being able to communicate with technical experts and understand their jargon. It also includes the ability to judge their work and perhaps even to reject it as being of poor quality or little value.

The book does not attempt to turn managers into complete forecasting experts. Forecasting is a tricky business and even with the increasing number of excellent computer packages now available, experience and technical knowledge are still required. What we hope to do is give you the confidence to get involved. This is the best way to gain experience. If you want to do your own forecasting, either because you have your own microcomputer or because you work for a small organization where expert help is out of the question, the book provides the basic concepts essential for a more advanced technical study.

The first chapter gives a management context for business forecasting. By providing a nine-point checklist for managing a forecasting system, it outlines the action a manager needs to take to make forecasts effective.

The next three chapters deal with techniques. A manager does not need to know the full mathematical and technical detail of every forecasting technique available. But he does need to know enough about the concepts and principles to be able to communicate with the experts. He may also need to understand the essentials of computer output. A manager who lacks this understanding may opt out of discussions with experts because he has no idea of the principles being discussed or because he is confused by the jargon. As a result, his expertise is lost to the forecasting project. Knowledge of the underlying concepts gives the manager the confidence to take part in such discussions. Chapters 2–4 try to achieve the delicate balance between too much and too little technical detail. Too little, and only a shallow understanding of the concepts results; too much, and the important concepts are obscured by the less important technicalities.

Chapters 5–7 are concerned with the management aspects of forecasting. These include relating forecasts to decisions and appraising forecasts, as well as implementing and monitoring them. These are all areas which definitely fall within the responsibility of the manager rather than that of the technical expert. Chapter 7 concerns the things a manager needs to do in order to make business forecasts work. When a manager, for whatever reasons, opts out of the forecasting process, these topics are, by default, left to the technical experts. Consequently the necessary action is frequently not taken and whole dimensions of forecasting systems can sometimes be ignored.

Chapters 8 and 9 are case studies, bringing together many of the ideas described in the book. The first case shows how a microcomputer can be used to assist a company with financial forecasting; the second illustrates how the setting up of a forecasting system can be based on the nine-point checklist. The final chapter deals with data sources for forecasting. It describes and lists sources of data and, where necessary, the means to access them. The chapter distinguishes between raw data (such as annual accounts or government statistics) and more refined data (including ready-made forecasts of the United Kingdom economy).

The whole book should be approached as an exploration of what a manager should know and what he or she can do to make a business-forecasting system of real practical value within an organization. It is intended to provoke thought, as well as to inspire action. The section on Further Reading indicates the directions in which an interest in forecasting can be developed.

CHAPTER 1

The Context of Business Forecasting

The business world of the 1960s and earlier was more stable than it is at present. This view is not merely the product of nostalgic reminiscence: business and economic data of the period reveal relatively smooth series with steady variations through time. As a result, business forecasting was not the issue it is now. In fact, many managers claim to have done their forecasting on the back of the proverbial envelope. The situation is different today. Uncertainty is evident everywhere in the business world. Forecasting has become more and more difficult. Data, whether from companies, industries or nations, seem to be increasingly volatile. The rewards for good forecasting are very high; the penalties for bad forecasting or for doing no forecasting at all are greater than ever. Even the most non-numerate managers tend to agree that a second envelope is insufficient.

As a consequence, interest and investment in forecasting methods have been growing. Organizations are spending more time and money on their planning. Much of this increased effort has gone into techniques. Established techniques are being used more widely; new techniques have been developed. The specialist forecaster's role has grown. Unfortunately, the outcome of all this effort has not always been successful. Indeed, some of the most costly mistakes in business have been made because of the poor use of forecasting methods. Analysing these mistakes reveals that in the main they came about not through technical errors, but because of the way the forecasting was organized and managed.

While attention has rightly been given to the 'kitbag of techniques' of the practitioner (statistician, operational researcher etc.), the roles of non-specialists involved in the process (general managers, accountants, financial analysts, marketing experts and those who are to use the forecasts to take decisions) have been neglected. These roles are usually concerned with managing the forecasts. However, because they have less technical expertise, the non-specialists have tended to hold back and not participate in planning and operating the forecasting system. Their invaluable (although non-statistical) expertise is thereby lost to the organization. Accordingly, the effectiveness of many organizations' forecasting work has been seriously weakened. The role of the non-specialist is at least as important as that of the practitioner.

The purpose of this chapter is to describe the role of managers and non-specialists in the forecasting process and to show what they can do to improve the forecasting performance of the organization. This chapter will also provide a context for the more detailed topics later in the book.

The Manager's Role in Managing Forecasts

Who Should Be In Charge?

In small organizations forecasting may be done by one person. The individual who needs the forecasts has to produce them. He has to cover all aspects of the work himself.

In larger organizations the question arises as to which department should take overall responsibility. There are three general possibilities:

User department

Managment services

Data processing unit

The third possibility, data processing, is perhaps the most popular, but probably the worst, candidate. The user department may well abrogate its responsibility to the 'experts' and as a result never become involved. While the members of the data processing unit will have plenty of technical expertise, they will know little of the wider issues and will be unable to integrate the forecasting system with the decision taking it is intended to serve. The most likely outcome is an isolated and little-used forecasting system.

The second possibility, management services, suffers from some of the problems of the data processing unit in being remote from the decision taking. Yet when the forecasts are for strategic decisions at board level this solution can be successful. Management services, perhaps in the form of a corporate planning unit, is then able to devote itself entirely to the major decisions to be taken. It can make the link between the technicalities of forecasting and the decisions.

The first possibility, the user department, should be the best solution for non-board level decisions. However, it frequently does not work. The users feel they have insufficient technical expertise and therefore hand over responsibility to the technical experts in another department. As a result they have little involvement in the system which once again may lead to it being under-utilized. Bringing forecasting non-specialists into the process and maintaining their participation is a key factor for the future of business forecasting. The non-specialists are in the best position to forge the link between techniques and decisions.

Wherever responsibility rests, accountants usually play a part. Frequently the forecasts are financial and accountants are involved as members of the user department. Even when the forecasting is centred on, say, marketing or production control, there are likely to be financial aspects to be considered and financial expertise will be required.

In larger organizations, therefore, forecasting is generally a team activity. Typically, the team members will be a forecasting practitioner, a representative of the user department and a financial expert, although the exact composition inevitably depends upon individual circumstances. In small organizations the forecasting may be done by one person in whom must be combined all the team's expertise. That person is likely to be someone in a general management position.

In a team, the role of the practitioner is reasonably clear. The roles of the other team members include facilitating access to the user department and providing financial data, but, much more importantly, they must include responsibility for 'managing' the forecasts. This means ensuring that resources (the forecasts) are properly applied to objectives (the intended uses of the forecasts). In carrying this out, it is essential to view forecasting as a system and not just as a technique. While the specialist is considering the statistical niceties of the numbers being generated, the manager should be considering the links with the rest of the organization: what is the decision-taking system which the forecasts are to serve? is the accuracy sufficient for the decisions being taken? are the forecasts being monitored and the methods adjusted? and so on. In short the specialist takes a *narrow* view of the technique but the manager takes a *broad* view of the whole forecasting system. The role of managing the system frequently falls, often by default, to a manager in the user department. It is the most vital role in the forecasting process.

What Do You Need To Know?

The recommended broad view can be broken down into three distinct areas. They show the non-specialist knowledge with which a manager needs to be equipped in order to play an effective part in the system.

Being aware of the range of techniques available. A specialist may have a 'pet' technique. The manager should have a good general knowledge of the full spectrum of techniques so that he can make at least an initial judgement on whether they apply to his situation. Such knowledge will also increase his confidence and credibility when taking part in discussions with specialists.

Incorporating forecasts into management systems. This is the essence of the manager's role. A checklist of things which should be done to integrate a forecasting process with the rest of the organization will be described later in the chapter.

Being aware of past forecasting errors. Many organizations have made forecasting errors in the past. Most have one thing in common: they are sufficiently simple that, with hindsight, it seems remarkable that the mistakes could have been made. Yet the errors were made and they are a source of valuable information for the present.

These three areas will now be amplified. Practical examples will be used to pinpoint the nature of a manager's contribution in managing a forecasting system and to confirm the importance of this task.

The Main Forecasting Techniques

This review describes in outline different approaches to forecasting and provides some general awareness of the range of techniques available. The details will be given in later chapters. Forecasting techniques can be divided into three categories:

Qualitative

Causal modelling

Time series methods

Qualitative methods are based on judgement rather than records of past data. Popular opinion might suggest that qualitative methods are the best. Stories abound of managers with 'instinct' who made predictions with astounding accuracy. On the other hand, the few surveys which have been done show that qualitative methods are, in general, inferior to quantitative ones. The reason for this anomaly may be psychological. There is a tendency to remember the successes of people and forget their failures. The man who predicted policitical revolution in Iran in 1979 is remembered, while the man who said that sliced bread would never catch on is forgotten. The opposite seems to be the case with systems: successes are forgotten, failures remembered.

Even so, some qualitative techniques have a successful record. These are the ones which convert judgements into forecasts in a thoughtful and systematic manner. They are different from the instant guesses which are often thought of as qualitative forecasts. More importantly, there are many situations where the qualitative approach is the only one possible. For new products, industries or technologies (developing and retailing microcomputer software, for instance) no past records are available to predict future business; in some countries political uncertainties may mean that past records are not valid. In these situations qualitative techniques provide **systematic** ways of making forecasts. Qualitative techniques will be the subject of chapter 2.

Causal modelling means that the variable to be forecast is related statistically to one or more other variables which are thought to 'cause' changes in it. The relationship is assumed to hold in the future and is used to make the forecasts. For example, the well-known econometric forecasts of national economies are based on causal modelling relating one economic variable to another. Policies, such as restricting the money supply, and economic assumptions, such as the future price of oil, are fed into the model to give forecasts of inflation, unemployment etc. A further example might be a company trying to predict its turnover on the basis of advertising expenditure, product prices and economic growth. The value of causal modelling is that it introduces, statistically, external factors into the forecasting. This type of method is therefore usually good at discerning turning points in a data series. Causal modelling will be the subject of chapter 3.

Time series methods predict future values of a variable solely from historical values of itself. They involve determining patterns in the historical record and then projecting the patterns into the future. While these methods are not good when the underlying conditions of the past are no longer valid, there are many circumstances when time series methods are the best. They are used when:

1 Conditions are stable and will continue to be so in the future.
2 Short-term forecasts are required and there is not enough time for conditions to change more than a little.
3 A base forecast is needed onto which can be built changes in future conditions.

Time series methods are also usually the cheapest and easiest to apply and can therefore be used when there are many forecasts to be made, none of which warrants a large expenditure. This might be the case in forecasting stock levels at a warehouse dealing in large numbers of small-value items. Time series methods will be the subject of chapter 4.

Developing A System

The key word is *system*. Forecasting should not be viewed as a number-generating technique but as a system. The technique is just one part of the forecasting process which includes many other factors to do with the generation and use of forecasts within an organization. The process should specify how judgement is to be incorporated, how the effectiveness of the forecasts is to be measured, how the system should be adjusted in response to feedback and many other aspects. In addition, a broad view leads to consideration of the links between the forecasting system and other management systems in the organization. Lack of thought about the nature of these links is often the reason why forecasts may be accurate yet ineffective.

Gwilym Jenkins, father of one of the most sophisticated modern forecasting techniques, suggested some guidelines for the development of a forecasting system.

1 *Analyse the decision-making systems* to be served by the forecasts. This involves listing and describing all decisions and actions influenced by the forecasts, the people involved and the links between them. For instance, forecasts of car sales may be required by the manager of an assembly line at a car plant. Primarily, the forecasts will help decide the speed and mix of the line (the total volume produced and the split between different variants of the model). But other decisions will be influenced by the forecasts: the ordering of steel, the production of

sub-assemblies, the buying of components and the setting of stock levels for example. Forecasts for the assembly line should not be made without a thorough analysis of their impact on other areas. The analysis may reveal fundamental flaws in decision systems or organizational structure which must be sorted out before any forecasts stand a chance of being effective. This is a lengthy but essential process.

2 *Define what forecasts are needed.* This comprises determining forecast variables, frequencies, time horizons and accuracy levels. In the car assembly example it might imply forecasting total demand and variant mix weekly for eight weeks ahead. No more than a medium level of accuracy would probably be required because stocks provide a balancing factor. Defining the forecasts like this prevents the generation of needless forecasts (over-accurate, too frequent, covering too great a time horizon). It can only be done after the decision process has been analysed because, for instance, the ordering of steel may require a greater time horizon than is strictly necessary for the assembly line alone. Some important aspects of the link between forecasts and decisions will be the subject of chapter 5.

3 *Develop a conceptual model* of the forecasting method. This suggests the ideal forecasting method and includes all the factors which might be suspected of affecting the variable being forecast. It indicates the historical patterns which might influence the future, causal variables and whether volatile conditions might point to the use of a qualitative method. In the car assembly example the factors might include seasonal patterns, the economic environment, marketing activity levels, stock levels and price changes. The development of a conceptual model causes thought to be given to the realities of a situation. It should prevent a blind rush into inappropriate statistical techniques.

4 *Ascertain the data available* (and those not available). This will indicate the ways in which the actual forecasting method might fall short of the ideal. It might be impossible to split advertising and promotional expenditures or difficult to measure stock levels accurately. Both these factors would affect the car production forecasting method by limiting the variables that could be included. Sources of data will be the subject of chapter 10.

5 *Develop the actual method* for making forecasts. This is the technique part of the system, involving the selection of a suitable technique

based on the forecasts, accuracy required and the data and resources available. In many organizations it is the only part of the system given any real consideration. The chosen method for car demand might be a causal model (relating demand to an economic variable, perhaps personal disposable income, and marketing variables, perhaps relative price and promotional expenditure) but with an allowance for seasonal effects. Chapters 2 to 4 deal with techniques and their relative advantages.

6 *Test the method's accuracy.* At this stage several techniques might be on the shortlist. They must be compared on the basis of past data and the best chosen for use. The tests involve some statistical ideas to be described in chapter 6.

7 *Decide how to incorporate judgements* into the forecasts. Quantitative forecasting models work on the assumption (not always explicitly recognized) that many of the conditions of the past will continue to prevail in the future. This is true for causal modelling just as for time series modelling. The influence of the economic environment on car demand, for example, may be assumed to apply as in the past. Other factors, such as political circumstances, may mean that the future is radically different from the past. It may not be possible to quantify these factors. Qualitative views about such changes should be allowed to influence the forecast. Of course, a remarkably large number of people believe strongly that they have special insights denied to other managers. It is not being suggested here that free rein should be given to the making of instinctive and arbitrary changes.

A systematic method for incorporating judgement should be developed. This may lean on one of the qualitative forecasting methods. It will certainly require people to be accountable for the changes they make. In the car example the plant manager may take the view that industrial problems are brewing at a rival car maker and that demand may increase as a consequence of the rival's inability to supply. There should be a means of testing his view and, if it seems valid, of allowing it to influence the forecast. If a forecasting method does not allow for such changes then the decision takers may disregard the forecasts and go their own way. The whole system may then lose credibility and fall into disuse. Chapter 7 goes into more detail on ways of incorporating judgements into forecasts.

8 *Implement the forecasting system.* This means ensuring in the initial stages that the system is being properly used, correcting problems

and answering queries. It is essential that when the system is first used, the designers of the system are available for advice and to check that its operation is understood. Chapter 7 gives more details.

9 *Monitor the performance* of the forecasting system. The operation of the system should be checked continually to verify that all is happening according to the specification, both in terms of the use being made of the system and in its statistical performance. Tests of the accuracy of the forecasts should be made with a view to changing the technical structure of the model as conditions change, and improving the accuracy (rather than allocating blame or giving praise). This topic will also receive further attention in chapter 7.

The checklist provides the context in which to view the later chapters. In particular, the final case study, in chapter 9, demonstrates specifically how the checklist can be the basis for tackling a forecasting problem.

To reiterate, a broad view of forecasting must be taken. The reason for discussing forecasting as a system and giving a nine-point checklist is that forecasting seems to fail in organizations far more often because of poor management of the forecasting process than because of technical errors. Some examples of errors which have occurred are the subject of the next section.

Forecasting Errors – Famous Mistakes

The history of business forecasting is crowded with expensive mistakes. Some cases are presented here with the positive purpose of learning from others. The mistakes are a guide to the surprisingly simple and usually non-technical things that can and do go wrong.

Chartering Oil Tankers

In his book *Practical Experiences with Modelling and Forecasting Time Series* Gwilym Jenkins cites the case of an oil company which lost enormous sums of money by taking too superficial an approach to forecasting. A time series approach was adopted which was unsuited to the circumstances.

Figure 1 shows the spot prices for chartering oil tankers for the years 1968–71. Analysing the series and detecting an upwards trend in 1969 and early 1970, it was assumed that the trend would continue,

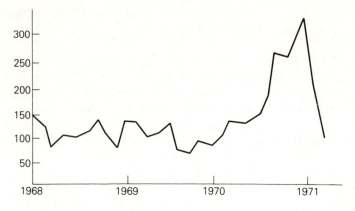

Figure 1.1   Spot price for chartering tankers, 1968–71.

at least in the short term. The company could therefore save money
by current rather than future chartering. Accordingly, charter contracts were taken out. The spot price continued to rise; more contracts
were arranged. No doubt other oil companies, noticing what was
happening, became involved. The spot price rose to great heights.
When the chartering activity came to a halt in early 1971, the spot
price fell to its pre-1970 level. Contracts taken out at this time would
have been at about one-third the price of just a few months earlier.
The cost to the company of the over-priced contracts has been
estimated at £250 million.

Two mistakes had been made. First, the company's intervention in
the spot market affected the market mechanism and thus the price.
This occurred because the company was very large and because the
supply of oil tankers is, in the short term, fixed. This is a conceptual
error, which with the benefit of hindsight can be seen with some
clarity. The second mistake was more technical. A deeper analysis of
the series would have revealed that it had the appearance of a
'random walk': the step from one spot price to the next seemed to be a
random one. If it was random, then by definition there was no
pattern in the movement of the spot prices. This would mean that
time series analysis was inapplicable. The basis of time series analyses
is that they determine patterns in historical data and project them into
the future. If there are no patterns, then time series analysis will fail.
Worse still, any patterns determined in subsets of the data will be
spurious and may lead to false conclusions.

In the absence of patterns in the series, a different type of forecasting method should be employed. In this case a causal approach would have been better. An investigation of factors likely to cause the spot price to vary, such as supply of tankers, demand for oil and economic variables, would have had a better chance of bearing fruit.

Airline Passenger Miles

Distinguishing between the statistical and non-statistical aspects of forecasting, and thinking clearly about both, might have saved an airline from an expensive and embarrassing error. One Sunday the planning director of the airline noticed a graph of the Index of UK Manufacturing Production in the business supplement of his Sunday newspaper. The thought struck him that the shape of the graph was very much the same as that of 'Passenger Miles Flown' with his airline. On Monday he set his team to work and they developed a causal model linking the two variables. Analysis showed that, statistically, the model was a good one and it was subsequently used to predict future business. It was several months later when it started producing unsatisfactory forecasts and had to be abandoned.

There were two mistakes in this piece of forecasting. First, the strong statistical evidence had demonstrated only that the two variables were *associated*. It had not shown that the link was *causal*. Over the period of analysis both variables had risen steadily as the UK economy slowly grew. When the economic situation changed, manufacturing production dropped. At the same time the $/£ exchange rate increased and large numbers of tourists flew off to the USA for holidays. Consequently Passenger Miles Flown increased at a time when the model was predicting a decrease. There was no causal link between the variables so, when circumstances altered, the model no longer held good.

The second mistake was that in order to forecast Passenger Miles Flown the airline had first to forecast the Index of Manufacturing Production. This in itself was no trivial matter. A direct attempt at forecasting Passenger Miles Flown would have carried an equal chance of success while saving time and effort. Where forecasts of economic variables are needed, ones which are readily available should be chosen. Good forecasts of some economic variables, such as gross domestic product, personal disposable income and others are published regularly by a variety of econometric forecasting institutes.

Production Planning – Where A Forecast Wasn't Used

Forecasts are not always monitored for accuracy after the event. A company in the manufacturing industry did check its sales forecasting accuracy and found that the predictions were excellent. However, the production planning for which the forecasts were prepared was poor. After investigation it was found that the forecasts, delivered each week in the form of large, heavy computer printouts, were never used. The production planners could not understand the output and no-one ever explained the printout to them. They ignored it and used their own judgemental forecasts which were poor (just how poor the production planners did not realize until they were monitored). The fault lay with the designers of the forecasting system. They should have produced their output in a form the users could understand and discussed its use with those who received it. The forecasting had never been integrated with the decision making it was intended to serve.

Stories of errors in forecasting are usually about inaccurate forecasts being used, with disastrous results. An equally frequent occurrence may be as in the above example, when accurate forecasts are not used, with disastrous results.

These three examples show how easily major mistakes can be made. More especially, they show that the role of the forecasting non-specialist in supervising a forecasting effort or as part of a forecasting team is of vital importance. Mistakes are usually non-technical in nature. There is no guaranteed means of avoiding them but it is clearly the responsibility of the managers in the team to guard against them. The lessons which other organizations have learned the hard way can help them in their task.

Doing Your Own Forecasting

Managers have a clear role in managing forecasts. The advent of microcomputers (desk-top computers) has made it easier for them to become practitioners of forecasting as well. Management journals have recently been reporting this phenomenon. The low cost of a fairly powerful microcomputer means that it is not a major acquisition; software (the programs) and instruction manuals are readily available. With a small investment in time and money, managers, frustrated by delays and apparent barriers around specialist departments, take the initiative and are soon generating forecasts themselves. They can use their own data to make forecasts for their own decisions without having to work through management services or data processing units.

This development has several benefits. The link between technique and decision is made more easily; one person has overall understanding and control; time is saved; reforecasts are quickly obtained.

But of course there are pitfalls. There may be no common database, no common set of assumptions within an organization. For instance, an apparent difference between two capital expenditure proposals may have more to do with data/assumption differences than with differences between the profitability of the projects. Another pitfall is in the use of statistical techniques which may not be as straightforward as the software manual suggests. The use of techniques with no knowledge of when they can or cannot be applied is dangerous. A time series method applied to a random data series (such as chartering oil tankers) is an example. The computer will always (well, nearly always) give an answer. Whether it is legitimate to base a business decision on it is another matter.

Later chapters dealing with technical aspects are intended to help the microcomputer user avoid fundamental errors as well as to provide the manager of a forecasting system with an overview of techniques. The case study presented in chapter 8 is based on the use of a microcomputer to make forecasts.

Conclusion

This chapter has advised that the management aspects of forecasting are too often neglected and should be given more prominence. Statistical theory and techniques are of course important as well, but the disproportionate amounts of time spent studying and discussing them gives a wrong impression of their value in relation to other considerations.

One piece of advice might be to avoid forecasting. Sensible people should only use forecasts, not make them. The general public and the world of management judges forecasts very harshly. Unless they are exactly right, they are thought to be failures. And they are never exactly right. This rigid and unrealistic test of forecasting is unfortunate. The real test is whether the forecasting is, on average, better than the alternative, which is often a guess – frequently, not even an educated guess.

A more positive view is that the present time is a particularly rewarding one to invest in forecasting. The volatility in data series seen since the mid-1970s puts a premium on good forecasting. At the same time, facilities for making good forecasts are now readily available in the form of a vast range of techniques and a wide choice of relatively cheap microcomputers. With the latter, even sophisticated forecasting methods can be applied to large data sets. It can all be done on a manager's desk-top without his having to engage in lengthy discussions with experts in other departments of his organization.

Whether the manager is doing the forecasting himself or is part of a team, he can make a substantial contribution to forward planning. To do so, he needs to arm himself with some background information and to be aware of the hidden traps.

CHAPTER 2

Qualitative Forecasting

Qualitative forecasting techniques are not based on numerical data. They are methods of combining qualitative information such as experience, judgement and intuition to make a forecast. Qualitative information can be slippery. Unless it is handled carefully the forecasts will be little more than wild guesses. Consequently, the essence of the techniques is that they are systematic. The best techniques are able to distil the real information in, say, a manager's experience from the surrounding 'noise' of personality and group pressures, directing it to the making of forecasts. For example, the Delphi technique is a way of obtaining a forecast from a group of people without the process being influenced by the usual group pressures of character strength, function in the organization and status.

Qualitative forecasting uses a different approach from that of quantitative forecasting. The former is more concerned with defining the boundaries or directions in which the future will lie; the latter is concerned with making estimates of the future values of variables. For example, qualitative techniques might predict the most profitable product areas and countries of operation for an organization, whereas quantitative techniques would try to forecast the actual levels of profit. This may make it seem as if the quantitative techniques are clearly superior. An old (and possibly true) forecasting story demonstrates that this is not necessarily so. In 1880 it was forecast that by 1920 London would be impassable to traffic under a three-foot layer of horse manure. Qualitative techniques might have avoided this error by considering changes in the technology of road transport corresponding to the fast-developing railway network.

This last example also illustrates why qualitative forecasting is sometimes referred to as technological forecasting. In this sense, qualitative techniques try to predict turning points and new directions of business activity. The fact that the business environment is rapidly changing and that there is a corresponding need to forecast technological change is undoubtedly behind the recent increase in the use of these techniques. And of course there are situations in which the lack of quantitative data means that qualitative techniques are all that can be used.

This chapter looks first at the sort of situations in which qualitative techniques are used. It then goes on to describe several such techniques. Those included are by no means an exhaustive list, nor are they necessarily the ones most frequently used. Rather, they are intended to convey the scope of the techniques available. Many qualitative techniques are at an early stage of development and the extent of their application is unclear. The advantages and disadvantages of qualitative techniques are discussed at the end of the chapter.

Where Qualitative Techniques Are Successful

People appear naturally to associate formal organizational forecasting with quantitative rather than qualitative techniques. Forecasting is seen as a numerical and analytical process. What then causes organizations to act 'unnaturally' and use qualitative techniques? And why is the use of these techniques increasing so rapidly? Two motives lie behind the use of qualitative techniques.

The first motive is that the forecaster's choice is restricted because there is a lack of adequate data. Quantitative techniques work from an historical data record, and preferably a long one. A lack of data may occur simply because no records exist. The organization may be marketing an entirely new product or exporting to a region in which it has no experience. Alternatively, data may exist but be inadequate. This may be because data have been recorded incompetently; more likely, it will be because the circumstances in which the data are generated are changing rapidly. For example, the political situation in an importing country may be unstable, making past records of business an unreliable base for future projections. Recently this problem has been seen in situations affected by rapidly changing technology. In microcomputing events happen so quickly that historical data are soon out of date. For example, forecasts of microcomputer software sales are difficult to make quantitatively because product developments occur so frequently and the rate of growth of sales is so steep. Quantitative techniques are generally poor at dealing with situations which are developing so quickly.

The second motive for using qualitative techniques is a more positive one: the factors affecting the forecast may be better handled qualitatively. Recall from chapter 1 that an important step in a systematic approach to forecasting is a conceptual model in which the influences on the forecast are listed. The most important influences may be ones which are not easily quantified. Such influences could give rise to quantum leaps in the forecast variable. For example, forecasts of business activity in Hong Kong must be influenced in a major way by the agreement between the United Kingdom and the Republic of China on the colony's future. The nature of this agreement and the way it is implemented would be difficult to deal with quantitatively, yet nothing is likely to have a greater bearing on future business activity. It would probably be better to try to estimate the effect of this influence qualitatively. It is therefore by no means always the case that qualitative techniques are a second-best to quantitative ones; in some situations they will better reflect actual circumstances.

These are the two motives for using qualitative techniques. The other question posed at the outset concerned the increasing frequency of their use. The answer lies in the second of these motives. The business environment seems recently to have been changing more rapidly than previously, whether for technological or political reasons. The situations in which qualitative techniques are seen to have advantages are occurring more frequently. The micro-electronic revolution is a clear example of this, but the boundaries are wider. Since the late 1970s business data have tended to be more volatile than previously. Many data series show greater variability in recent years. This has meant that the rewards for accurate forecasting have increased, but it also means that previously established forecasting models have performed less well. The need to plan successfully and the need to consider new techniques have resulted in greater use of forecasting techniques, in terms both of the number of organizations that have a forecasting system and of the range of techniques employed.

The next section outlines some of the major qualitative forecasting techniques and gives examples.

Qualitative Techniques

Several of the most common qualitative forecasting methods hardly deserve the title technique, although they have been given pseudo-scientific labels. They are included here if only for the sake of completeness before moving on to more serious contenders.

Visionary forecasting involves a purely subjective estimate (or guess, or hunch, or stab in the dark) made by one individual. Many managers believe themselves to be good at this; or they believe that someone else in the organization is good at it. Most organizations like to believe that they have a forecasting hero tucked away on the third floor. Sadly, when these forecasts are properly monitored, the records usually show visionary forecasting to be inaccurate. The reason for this paradox seems to be that visionary forecasting is judged on its occasional successes. Everyone remembers when someone, in 1978, predicted political changes in Iran; the occasion when another individual stated that the \$/£ exchange rate would never fall below 1.50 is forgotten. By contrast, scientific methods tend to be judged by their occasional failures. For example, in 1982 econometric forecasts of exchange rates by leading institutions were badly wrong. This is generally remembered, whereas the success of econometrics at most other times both in forecasting and policy making tends to be forgotten. There are undoubtedly people who are good visionaries, but they are few in number and their records should be carefully monitored.

Panel consensus forecasting is probably the most common method used in business. This refers to the meeting of a group of people who, as a result of argument and discussion, produce a forecast. One would think that this method should provide good forecasts, bringing together as it does the expertise of several people. Again, the record suggests otherwise. Panel consensus forecasts are generally inaccurate. The reason is that the forecasts are dominated by group pressures. The status, strength of character and vested interests of the participants all influence the forecast. The full potential of the gathered experience is not brought to bear and the forecast may turn out to be little different from that of the strongest personality working alone. Some improvement can be gained by using structured group meetings in which one person is given the responsibility for organizing the meeting and providing background information.

Brainstorming is a technique perhaps better known for producing ideas rather than generating forecasts. It is based on a group meeting, but with the rule that every suggestion must be heard. No proposal is to be ridiculed or put aside without discussion. In forecasting, brainstorming is used first to define the full range of factors which influence the forecast variable and then to decide upon a forecast. When properly applied it is a useful technique but the process can degenerate into an ill-disciplined panel consensus forecast.

Market research also falls within the area of qualitative forecasting. It is an accurate but expensive technique. This extensive subject involves a large number of distinct skills such as statistical sampling, questionnaire design and interviewing. It is more usually described in the context of marketing.

The techniques described in more detail below are potentially effective and accurate as well as falling firmly within the area of qualitative forecasting.

Delphi Forecasting

Named after the oracle of Ancient Greece, this technique is based upon the panel consensus method but tries to overcome the ill-effects of group pressures. It does this by not allowing the members of the group to communicate with one another. The group can therefore be physically in the same place or at the end of telephones. The group has a chairman who conducts proceedings. The process is as follows:

1 The chairman asks each member of the group to make a forecast of the variable in question for the relevant time period. This forecast, along with an idea of what the participant believes are the major factors affecting the variable, are written down and passed (or phoned) to the chairman.
2 The chairman collects the submissions of all participants and summarizes them. A typical summary may comprise the average and range of the forecasts plus a list of the major factors. The chairman relays the summary back to the group. At no time are participants told anything about the individual response of other participants.
3 The chairman asks the group to reconsider their forecasts, taking into account the information presented to them in the summary. Again, the forecasts are submitted to the chairman for summary and relay.
4 The process is repeated until the group has reached (approximately) a consensus or until the participants are no longer prepared to adjust their forecasts further.
5 The **final result** is the Delphi forecast.

By keeping the participants apart, the intention is that effects such as personality and rank are minimized. The final forecast is then a distillation of the views of the entire group. Even better, each participant will have had the opportunity to re-adjust his views in response to worthy suggestions from others. The views of cranks, even persistent cranks, will be largely filtered out by the averaging process. The onus is on those deviating from the norm to defend their views.

When tested, the Delphi technique has produced good results. But it has some disadvantages. It can be expensive, especially when the group are assembled in the same physical place. Also, it is possible to cheat by indulging in some game playing: one participant, knowing the likely views of other participants can submit unrealistic forecasts in order that the averaging process works out as he wants. For example, in an attempt to forecast sales, a financial executive may substantially understate his view so that the optimistic view of the sales manager is counterbalanced; as a result, he achieves his aim of holding down stock levels.

The technique can be unreliable, since different groups of people might well produce different forecasts. The results can also be sensitive to the style of the questions posed to the group.

Scenario Writing

Scenario writing is not concerned with single estimates of the future. It is the construction of several sets of circumstances which could arise. Each set of circumstances is called a scenario and stems from a series of assumptions about the future. In other words, scenario writing is the translation of several different sets of assumptions into scenarios. The future is then represented by several alternative scenarios rather than one single view. The essence of scenario writing is the expression of a wide range of situations which could apply in the future and which describe the boundaries within which contingency planning can take place.

For example, suppose an exporting company is trying to forecast sales of its products in a South East Asian country in ten years' time. One set of assumptions could be that at that time there will be a pro-Western government and a strong world economy. In addition, there may be specific assumptions about inflation rates, exchange rates, technological changes etc. These assumptions are translated into a scenario which shows the sales, prices, costs, manpower and competition relating to the products. A second scenario is formed from a second and different set of assumptions. The process continues and more scenarios are formed until all sets of assumptions which could reasonably be expected to apply have been exhausted.

Scenario writing is not a detailed technique nor does it pretend to be accurate in terms of the numbers it produces. Rather, it involves a new approach to forecasting. The difficulty of making a definite forecast is recognized. Instead, the emphasis is on covering the range of possibilities and forming flexible plans which can cope with all of them. Its advantage is that it leads to a realistic perspective on future uncertainty. It can also be combined with more detailed techniques for translating assumptions into quantified scenarios. It is particularly useful in the most difficult type of forecasting, for example where the time horizon is long and there are many uncertainties.

By itself, of course, scenario writing is an approach rather than a technique. Nevertheless, in combination with other techniques, it is a highly constructive way of carrying out sensitivity analysis (asking 'what if?' questions).

Cross-Impact Matrices

Cross-impact matrices do not in themselves produce forecasts. They are a means of providing estimates of the likelihood or probabilities of future events which can then be used as part of the planning process. Special emphasis is placed on cross influences between different events, by considering how the occurrence of one event might affect the probability of another. Thus the technique gets its name: 'cross-impact'. The 'matrix' part of the name derives from the way the probabilities are written down, in a matrix.

The technique comprises the following steps. To illustrate, the previous example of a company forecasting its business activity in South East Asia will be used.

1 Make an extensive list of all the factors that might affect the plans to be made. In the example, this would include all the developments which could occur with regard to the political situation, the economic climate, technological breakthroughs, product innovation, competition and so on. For instance, three developments in the political situation might be used: a pro-Western, a Marxist or an independent government.

2 Estimate the probabilities of these developments. They would each have to be assessed subjectively using, perhaps, the Delphi method.

3 Form a matrix with each row representing one of the developments and each column also representing a development. Each element of the matrix is the new probability for the development in that

Table 2.1 A cross-impact matrix

If this development happens		Then the probability (%) of					
		A	B	C	D	E	F
Pro-Western govt.	(A)	—	0	0	50	40	10
Independent govt.	(B)	0	—	0	30	50	20
Marxist govt.	(C)	0	0	—	5	35	60
Economy grows 5%	(D)	30	65	5	—	0	0
Economy grows 1%	(E)	15	60	25	0	—	0
Economy declines	(F)	10	25	65	0	0	—

column given that the development of that row has taken place. In the example, a section of the completed matrix might appear as in table 2.1. No claim is made concerning the accuracy of the subjective probabilities in this example. The matrix is formed by taking the most likely development first and adjusting the probabilities of all the other developments. Then the second most likely development is taken, then the third and so on. If the most likely development is almost certain then the adjusted probabilities may be preferred in determining the second most likely.

4 Using the original probabilities and the cross probabilities, the overall likelihood of different developments can be calculated. This may involve simulation. For example, given the probabilities of all other developments, the relative frequency of occurrence of, say, the successful launch of some new, as yet non-existent, product can be calculated.

The essence of cross-impact matrices is that they are a means whereby the planner can juggle with a whole series of uncertain developments and in particular their influence on each other. The cost of the technique may only be justified when the list of developments is long. In these circumstances the whole process may be computerized, with formulae being the basis of the adjustment of the probabilities. How all the probabilities are used is not a part of the technique. They may be used formally in further calculations or they may be used informally in making judgements about the future. They may well be used as part of scenario writing to formulate the most realistic scenarios.

Although a sales example has been used to illustrate these steps, the technique is at its best when dealing with technological uncertainties. In fact, one of the earliest reports of its application was to the development of the US Minuteman missile system (Gordon and Hayward, 1968).

The advantage of the system is that it provides potential for the difficult task of dealing with a wide range of complex events and interactions in a relatively straightforward manner. Its disadvantages are that it is expensive, and that the forecaster must be capable of interpreting the probabilities produced.

Analogies

When forecasting a variable for which there is no data record, a second variable, whose history is completely known and which is supposed to be similar to the first, is used as an analogy. Because of conceptual similarities between the two, it is assumed that as time goes by the data pattern of the first will follow the pattern of the second. The forecast for the first is the already known history of the second.

For example, the company forecasting sales of a new product in South East Asia might choose as an analogy the sales of a previous new product with similar characteristics marketed in that country or a similar country in the recent past. The growth record of the previous product is the basis of the forecast for the current one. The forecast does not have to be exactly the same as the analogy. The record may be adjusted for level and scatter (or confidence limits). For instance, the sales volume of the current product may be thought to be double that of the previous one and to have greater month-by-month variations. To forecast, the growth record of the analogy would be doubled and the scatter of the monthly forecasts increased. The essence of the technique is not that the analogy should be exactly like the forecast variable but that similarities in the products and the marketing environment should be sufficient to believe that the data patterns will be comparable.

The advantage of the technique is that it provides a cheap but comprehensive forecast in a way that makes sense to the marketing managers. The analogy is not restricted to business. Biological growth can provide the basis for analogies in business and the social sciences. The underlying philosophy of the technique is that there may be social laws just as there are natural laws. Although the laws themselves in, say, marketing, may not be fully or even partially understood, data records are the evidence of the laws and can be used in forecasting.

The main problem with the technique is that there must be at least one but not too many analogies to choose from. If the situation is totally new to the organization there may not be an analogy. On the other hand, there may be several plausible analogies and great arguments may develop over deciding the right one to use. For example, a wine and spirits company was planning the launch of a new product about which high hopes were held. But it was extremely difficult to decide which of several previous successful products should be the analogy. All had been successful yet their growth patterns differed considerably. The problem was resolved by making a subjective decision in favour of one but agreeing to monitor the forecast variable's record closely to see if at some point the marketers should revert to a new analogy.

Catastrophe Theory

Most forecasting techniques, whether qualitative or quantitative, are based on the assumption that changes in the forecast variable will be, more or less, continuous. In other words although the variable may exhibit gradual trends or steep growth or decline, it will not jump from one level to another. Catastrophe theory deals with the possibility that a variable may jump from one level to another. It does not refer to catastrophe in the sense of disaster but in the sense of a sudden alteration in behaviour.

There are plenty of examples of this sort of behaviour in non-business fields: in psychology, the change of mood from, say, fear to anger; in chemistry, the changes in a substance from a solid to a liquid and from a liquid to a gas; in atomic physics, the ideas of quantum theory. In business the examples may not be so clear-cut but there are plenty of possibilities to think about: a rapid take-off in the sales of a product, a turn-around in a company's profitability, corporate failure, a sudden change in the price of a commodity. oil prices, Raw material

Catastrophe theory is not a quantitative technique. It does not calculate the expected size of jumps. Rather, it is a systematic way of determining whether a catastrophe is likely in a given situation. The technique comprises a series of questions to answer and characteristics to look for, which will indicate the nature of the situation being investigated.

Catastrophe theory is relatively new and there is not much in the way of a track record to judge its success. However, it certainly fills a gap in the range of forecasting techniques and is growing in popularity.

The reason for its importance and the interest it has created is that while companies can usually take emergency action to deal with continuous changes (whether rapid or not) in a situation, sudden jumps or reversions in behaviour often leave no time for evasive action. The potential of catastrophe theory is, then, that it may be able to predict circumstances with which companies have no way of dealing unless they have advance warning.

Relevance Trees

The techniques described so far have all started with the present situation and then put out 'feelers' to see what the future might look like. These techniques can be described as *exploratory*. The relevance trees technique is different. It starts in the future with a picture of what the future should ideally look like and works back to determine what must occur to make this future happen. Such an approach is described as *normative*.

The technique starts with a broad objective, breaks this down into sub-objectives, further breaks down the sub-objectives through, perhaps, several different levels until specific technological development is being considered. This structure is a relevance tree. The elements of the tree are then given relevance weights from which it is possible to calculate the overall relevance of the technological developments which are at the lowest level of the tree. The outcome of the technique is a list of those developments which are most important or relevant to the achievement of the higher level objective and sub-objectives.

There are seven steps in the application of relevance trees. They will be described using as an example a much simplified case of the design of a new passenger airliner.

1 Draw the relevance tree. For the airliner it might appear as in table 2.2 on p. 26.

2 Establish criteria for determining priorities. In a purely financial case there might be only one criterion – money. In the more usual technological applications there are several criteria which are the dimensions along which achievement can be measured. In the airliner example the criteria might be:

        A   Passenger comfort
        B   Safety
        C   Cost
        D   Route capability

Table 2.2   A relevance tree

Level   Objective: build commercially successful airliner

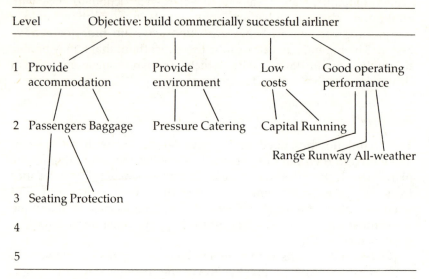

1 Provide   Provide   Low   Good operating
   accommodation   environment   costs   performance

2 Passengers Baggage   Pressure Catering   Capital Running

                                                    Range Runway All-weather

3 Seating Protection

4

5

3 Weight the importance of each criterion relative to the others. A group of experts would presumably have to carry out this task by answering questions such as: 'What is the weight of each criterion in achieving the highest level objective?' In the airliner example the weights might be assigned:

		weight
A	Passenger comfort	0.10
B	Safety	0.35
C	Cost	0.40
D	Route capability	0.15
		1.00

4 Weight the sub-objectives at each level (referred to as the elements of the tree) according to their importance in meeting each criterion. The question posed might be: 'In order to meet criterion C, what is the relative importance of each element at level 3?' At each level a set of weights for each criterion must be assessed. For the airliner example, the process might work as shown in table 2.3. The first column, for example, shows the assessed relevance of the four elements at level 1 to the criterion of comfort. Accommodation is weighted 0.20, environment 0.65 and so on. Since the table gives the relative relevance of the elements to the criteria, each column must

Table 2.3   Assessing a set of weights for each criterion at level 1

	Criteria			
	Comfort	Safety	Cost	Route
Criterion weight	0.10	0.35	0.40	0.15
Elements at level 1:	Element weights			
Accommodation	0.20	0.35	0.05	0.05
Environment	0.65	0.25	0.05	0.05
Low costs	0.05	0.05	0.75	0.25
Performance	0.10	0.35	0.15	0.65
	1.00	1.00	1.00	1.00

sum to 1. The process of assessing relevance weights is carried out for each level of the relevance tree.

5 Calculate partial relevance numbers. Each element has a partial relevance number (PRN) for each criterion. It is calculated:

$$PRN = \text{criterion weight} \times \text{element weight}$$

It is a measure of the relevance of that element with respect only to that criterion (hence 'partial'). For the airliner example the partial relevance numbers are shown in table 2.4. For instance, the PRN for accommodation with respect to comfort is:

$$0.2 \times 0.1 = 0.02$$

PRNs are calculated for each element at each level for each criterion.

6 Calculate a local relevance number (LRN) for each element. The LRN for each element is the sum of the PRNs for that element. It is a measure of the importance of that element relative to others at the same level in achieving the highest level objective. For the airliner example the LRNs are shown in table 2.5. The LRN for accommodation is 0.17 (= 0.0200 + 0.1225 + 0.0200 + 0.0075). There is one LRN for each element at each level.

7 Calculate cumulative relevance numbers (CRNs). There is one for each element. It is calculated by multiplying the LRN of an element by the LRNs of the each associated element at a higher level. This

Table 2.4   Calculating partial relevance numbers

	Criteria			
	Comfort	Safety	Cost	Route
Criterion weight	0.10	0.35	0.40	0.15
Elements at level 1:	Element weights			
Accommodation	0.20	0.35	0.05	0.05
Environment	0.65	0.25	0.05	0.05
Low costs	0.05	0.05	0.75	0.25
Performance	0.10	0.35	0.15	0.65
	Partial relevance numbers			
Accommodation	0.0200	0.1225	0.0200	0.0075
Environment	0.0650	0.0875	0.0200	0.0075
Low costs	0.0050	0.0175	0.3000	0.0375
Performance	0.0100	0.1225	0.0600	0.0975

Table 2.5   Calculating local relevance numbers

Level 1	Partial relevance numbers				LRN
Accommodation	0.0200	0.1225	0.0200	0.0075	0.17
Environment	0.0650	0.0875	0.0200	0.0075	0.18
Low costs	0.0050	0.0175	0.3000	0.0375	0.36
Performance	0.0100	0.1225	0.0600	0.0975	0.29

gives each element an absolute measure of its relevance. In the airliner example, at level 2 the CRN for seating is calculated:

$$\text{CRN (seating)} = \text{LRN (seating)} \times \text{LRN (passengers)} \times \text{LRN (accommodation)}$$

By this means the bottom row of elements (specific technological requirements) will have overall measures of their relevance in achieving the objective which was the starting point at the highest level of the tree. This should lead to decisions about the importance, timing, resource allocation etc. of the tasks ahead.

Remember that relevance trees is a normative technique. Given an objective it indicates what must be done to achieve it. It also indicates the relative importance or priorities of the tasks ahead. In doing so it suffers from two major disadvantages. The first is the requirement to draw a relevance tree correctly, comprehensively structuring the road ahead; the second is the subjective assessment of element and criterion weights. If either of these tasks is not done well, then the result will be nonsense. It is perhaps as well to look at relevance trees as much for the process of using the technique as for the final result. The activity of considering the options and their relevance would probably carry substantial benefits in terms of understanding future needs, even if the numerical relevance values were never to be used.

Conclusion

The obvious characteristic that distinguishes qualitative from quantitative forecasting is that the underlying information on which it is based consists of judgements rather than numbers. But the distinction goes beyond this. Qualitative forecasting is usually concerned with determining the boundaries within which the long-term future might lie; quantitative forecasting tends to provide specific point forecasts and ranges for variables in the nearer future. Qualitative forecasting offers techniques that are very different in type, from the straight-forward, exploratory Delphi method to the normative relevance trees. Also, qualitative forecasting is at an early stage of development and many of its techniques are largely unproven.

Whatever the styles of qualitative techniques, their aims are the same, to use judgements systematically in forecasting and planning. In using the techniques it should be borne in mind that the skills and abilities that provide the judgements are more important than the techniques. Just as it would be pointless to try a quantitative technique with 'made-up' numerical data, so it would be folly to use a qualitative technique in the absence of real knowledge of the situation in question. The difference is that it is perhaps easier to discern the lack of accurate data than the lack of genuine expertise.

On the other hand, where real expertise does exist it would be an equal folly not to make use of it. For long-term forecasting by far the greater proportion of available information about a situation is probably in the form of judgement rather than numerical data. To use these judgements without the help of a technique usually results in a plan or forecast biased by personality, group effects, self-interest etc. Qualitative techniques offer a chance to distil the real information from the surrounding noise and refine it into something useful.

In many, indeed most, forecasting problems the relevant information is both qualitative and quantitative. The most difficult task of all is to integrate these two types of information into a forecast. The first stage in the task is to recognize that the problem exists and that there is a great need to use both sources of data. The second stage is to solve the problem. Although not easy, it can be done. Some suggestions for tackling the problem are given in chapter 7, after quantitative techniques have been covered.

In spite of this enthusiasm for qualitative forecasting, the chapter must end with a warning. In essence, most qualitative techniques come down to asking questions of experts, albeit scientifically. Doubts about the value of experts are well entrenched in management folklore. But doubts about the questions can be much more serious, making all else pale into insignificance. Hauser (1975) reports the following extract from a survey of opinion.

Question	% answering yes
1 Do you believe in the freedom of speech?	96
2 Do you believe in the freedom of speech to the extent of allowing radicals to hold meetings and express their views to the community?	22

The lesson must be that the sophistication of the techniques will only be worthwhile if the forecaster gets the basics right first. This is especially true in qualitative forecasting.

CHAPTER 3

Causal Modelling

Causal modelling comprises those techniques in which the variable to be forecast is related statistically to one or more other variables which are thought to 'cause' changes in it. It is the means by which external influences on the forecast variable are measured. The statistical methods underlying causal modelling are *regression* and *correlation*. Regression is a method for determining the mathematical formula relating the variables; correlation is a method for measuring the strength of the relationship. Regression shows what the connection is; correlation shows whether it is strong enough to use.

For example, suppose a company wishes to predict the sales volume of a product. After due consideration of the relevant factors (stages 1–4 in the checklist in chapter 1), it is decided that the forecasting technique should be a causal model relating quarterly sales volume to quarterly advertising expenditure. If the historical records of both variables are plotted graphically the scatter diagram in figure 3.1 results. Each point refers to one quarter. For instance, the point A, at which $x = 12$ and $y = 36$, refers to the quarter when advertising expenditure was 12 (in £000) and sales volume was 36 (in 000).

From the scatter diagram it appears that there is a straight-line relationship between the variables. Regression will provide the mathematical formula linking them together. It might be:

sales volume = 21.3 + 1.1 × advertising expenditure

This formula could then be used to predict sales in a future quarter for which advertising expenditure had been decided. Note that even though it is being suggested that there is a linear relationship between sales and advertising, the points do not lie exactly on a straight line. When advertising expenditure = 12 is put into the equation sales volume does not equal 36 since A is not on the line. In

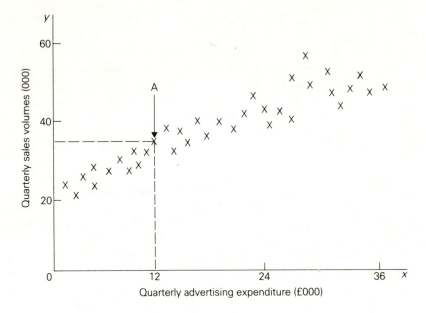

Figure 3.1   A scatter diagram relating quarterly sales and advertising.

this sense regression is an approximation. It is finding the best of many possible formulae which could link the variables.

While regression finds the formula, correlation will indicate the strength of the relationship. It will provide a measure of the extent to which the sales volume has moved in parallel with advertising expenditure in the past, i.e. whether a high level of sales in a quarter corresponded with a high advertising expenditure in the same quarter (and low with low). It will confirm the intuitive evidence of the scatter diagram.

The purpose of this chapter is to show how regression and correlation can be used in forecasting and to point out the pitfalls in their use. Initially, only simple linear regression will be described. Simple in this context means involving only two variables; linear means that the relationship is some form of straight line (as opposed to a curve). Later, the description will be extended to other types of regression. On the assumption that anyone doing causal modelling will have the help of some form of calculator or computer, the mathematics are kept to a minimum.

Where Causal Modelling is Successful

Potentially, causal modelling can be applied whenever movements in the variable to be forecast are thought to be influenced by other variables. Since most changes in variables are likely to be affected by some factors or other, this would seem to be a very broad category, covering most if not all forecasting situations. In practice, it is not so simple. Many circumstances can hinder the application of causal modelling. For example, the influencing factors might not be known, nor might it be worthwhile conducting lengthy investigations to uncover them. Also, causal modelling can be expensive to use, mainly because of all the data collection required. This may have to be considered when deciding whether to employ this approach. However, there are some clear pointers to those situations where causal modelling is likely to be successful.

The first is when there are *a priori* reasons for supposing that one variable is influenced by another. For instance, monetarist economists believe that the money supply has a direct bearing on inflation. It would therefore be sensible to use causal modelling to measure this relationship. In fact, most econometric forecasting is carried out through models based on such economic reasoning. Similarly, when making company forecasts, there will probably be sound reasons for basing them on the belief that advertising does affect sales levels.

Causal modelling is also suitable for the related situation in which a leading indicator is involved. As its name suggests, a leading indicator is a variable which precedes in time the forecast variable. For example. in forecasting the sales of children's clothing, the birth rate in earlier years might well be a leading indicator. Changes in the birth rate must surely affect the sales of children's clothing an appropriate number of years later. A causal model would relate sales to birth rate.

The real value of causal modelling is its potential for getting behind the numbers to the real causal influences. If this is done well, then turning points will be detected. In situations where there is a history of turning points or there is a likelihood of future ones, it may be worthwhile going to the expense of a causal modelling approach.

The time horizon (how far into the future the forecast extends) is also relevant. For the short term (a few months), delays in the causal effects as well as the time before new data are available will probably mean that it is not worthwhile trying to determine the causal influence. On the other hand for the long term (over ten years) there is always a possibility that causal effects may alter, raising doubts

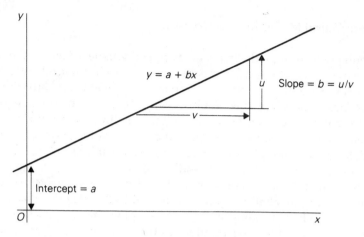

Figure 3.2(a)   The equation of a straight line; b is positive.

about the validity of this type of forecast. Causal modelling is often at its most useful in making medium-term (about five years) forecasts.

Nevertheless, there are no hard and fast rules for choosing the method to use. Each situation should be treated on its merits.

Mathematical Preliminaries

Simple linear regression refers to the case where two variables when plotted on a graph have an approximately straight-line relationship. Mathematically this means that the equation linking the variables is of the form:

$$y = a + bx \text{ (}bx\text{, or } b.x\text{, stands for } b \text{ multiplied by } x\text{)}$$

y and x are the variables; a and b are fixed numbers or constants. In the example above sales volume was y, advertising expenditure was x, a was 21.3 and b was 1.1.

Simple linear regression is the task of finding the values of a and b which provide the best connection between the two variables. As yet 'best' remains undefined.

The Equation of a Straight Line

The equation of a straight line is:

$$y = a + bx$$

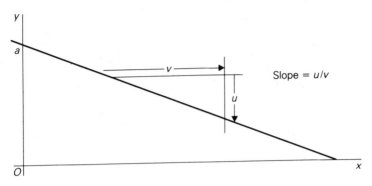

Figure 3.2(b)   The equation of a straight line; b is negative.

a is the *intercept*, the value of *y* at the point where the line crosses the *y* axis. This can be verified by noting that $y = a$ when $x = 0$.

b is the *slope*, the change in *y* for a change in *x* of one unit. A little algebra is needed to verify this fact.

In figure 3.2(a), an increase in *x* is associated with an increase in *y*, and *u* and *v* are therefore both positive. Consequently $b \, (= u/v)$ must be positive. In figure 3.2(b), an increase in *x* is associated with a decrease in *y*. Therefore while *v* is positive, *u* is negative. Consequently *b* must be negative.

Determining the equation of a straight line amounts to finding the values of *a* and *b*. Once *a* and *b* are known, the line is completely determined. Linear regression is the task of finding the values of *a* and *b* which provide the best connection between the two variables.

Residuals

Figure 3.3 is a scatter diagram. If any straight line is drawn through the set of points, the points will, in general, not fall exactly on a straight line. Consider the first point A, at $x = 1$. The *y* value at A is the actual *y* value. The point directly below A which lies on the line is B. The *y* value at B is the fitted *y* value. If the equation of the line is known, then the fitted *y* value is obtained by putting the *x* value at A into the equation and calculating *y*. This is the *y* value at B. If at A the actual *y* value is 12 and the line is $y = 10 + 0.5x$, the fitted *y* value is calculated:

$$\text{fitted } y \text{ value} = 10 + 0.5 \times 1 = 10.5$$

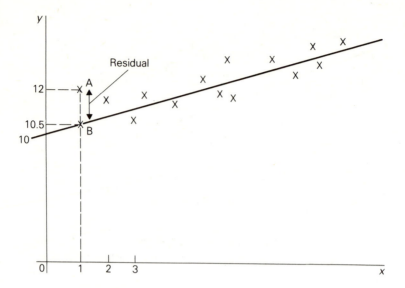

Figure 3.3   Calculating the residual for a given point.

The difference between actual and fitted *y* values is the residual.

$$\text{Residual} = \text{actual } y \text{ value} - \text{fitted } y \text{ value}$$

At A, the residual is $12 - 10.5 = 1.5$. If the point lies above the line, the residual is positive; if it is below, the residual is negative; if it is on the line, the residual is zero. Each point has a residual. The residuals would be different if a different line were drawn.

Simple Linear Regression

In deciding which straight line is the 'best' straight line through a set of points, a criterion is required. There must be some way of defining in what way 'best' is best. Since the line is to be close to the actual values (the points), the criterion should be something to do with making the residuals as small as possible. One approach would be to make the 'best' line the one for which the sum of the residuals is a minimum compared with any other line drawn through the points. This does not work, since positive and negative residuals will cancel out one another so that a line with large residuals can still have the sum of its residuals very small or even zero. Indeed, it can be proved

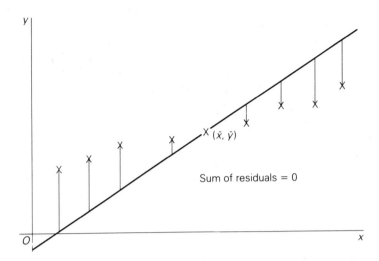

Figure 3.4   A line drawn through the mean values of x ($\bar{x}$) and y ($\bar{y}$) has the sum of its residuals equal to zero.

that any line through the mean value of x (usually labelled $\bar{x}$) and the mean value of y (usually labelled $\bar{y}$) will have the sum of its residuals equal to zero. (See figure 3.4.)

A second approach would be to make the sum of the absolute values of the residuals as small as possible. (The absolute value of a number is its size when the sign is ignored, for example the absolute value of $+6$ is $+6$, the absolute value of -6 is $+6$). This avoids the problem of positives and negatives cancelling. This would work well, except that the device of taking absolute numbers is not easy to manipulate mathematically. In the past, in the absence of efficient computers, this was an important consideration. For this reason the criterion has been rarely adopted, although the availability of computers has led to its being more widely used in recent years.

The third approach, and the one traditionally employed, is called least squares. The negative signs are eliminated by squaring the residuals (a negative number squared is positive). The sum of the squared residuals is a minimum for the 'best' line. In other words the 'best' line is the one which has values for a and b that make the sum of squared residuals as small as possible. The criterion in least-squares regression is:

$$\text{sum (residuals)}^2 \text{ is a minimum}$$

Least squares has some technical advantages over alternative criteria which will not be pursued here.

Once the least-squares criterion has been selected, it is not immediately obvious how it should be used to find the equation of the 'best' line. Finding the equation of the line means finding values for a and b in $y = a + bx$. The least-squares criterion has to be turned into formulae for calculating a and b. The means of the transformation is differential calculus, a level of mathematics beyond the scope of this text. Differential calculus will be left in its 'black box' and a jump made straight to the least-squares regression formulae:

for two variables, labelled x and y, and n paired observations on those variables, the least squares regression line is given by:

$$y = a + bx$$

$$\text{where } b = \frac{sum\ (x - \bar{x})\ (y - \bar{y})}{sum\ (x - \bar{x})^2}$$

$$\text{and} \quad a = \bar{y} - b\bar{x}$$

Fortunately the availability of computers and calculators means that these formulae rarely have to be used directly. To provide a better feel for regression, a simple example of the application of the formulae is given below.

Example. Find the regression line for the points:

x	1	2	4	5	8	mean $(\bar{x}) =$ 4
y	20	19	34	30	47	mean $(\bar{y}) =$ 30

Sum $(x - \bar{x})\ (y - \bar{y}) = (1 - 4)\ (20 - 30) + (2 - 4)\ (19 - 30) + (4 - 4)\ (34 - 30) + (5 - 4)\ (30 - 30) + (8 - 4)\ (47 - 30)$
$$= 30 + 22 + 0 + 0 + 68$$
$$= 120$$

sum $(x - \bar{x})^2$
$$= (1 - 4)^2 + (2 - 4)^2 + (4 - 4)^2 + (5 - 4)^2 + (8 - 4)^2$$
$$= 9 + 4 + 0 + 1 + 16$$
$$= 30$$

From the 'black box' formulae:

$b = 120/30$
$\quad = 4$

$a = 30 - (4 \times 4)$
$\quad = 14$

The regression line is therefore:

$y = 14 + 4x$

Correlation

The formulae for a and b can be applied to any set of data. The scatter diagram may show that the points lie approximately on a circle but regression will still find the 'best' line. Correlation will quantify the strength of the relationship and help decide whether, in view of the closeness (or otherwise) of the points to a line, the regression line will be of any practical use. If the variables have not had a linear relationship in the past it would not make sense to use such a relationship for forecasting the future.

The strength of the relationship is measured by the *correlation coefficient* (denoted by r). It can take on all values between -1 and $+1$. Figure 3.5 illustrates the meaning of different values.

Correlation coefficients close to -1 or $+1$ always indicate a strong relationship between the variables. Close to zero, they indicate a weak relationship. An intuitive understanding of the way the correlation coefficient works can be gained by considering the correlation coefficient squared. By convention, and for no apparent reason, it is written with a capital letter, R^2. The explanation is as follows.

Before carrying out a regression analysis the total variation in the y variable can be measured by:

$$\text{total variation} = \text{sum } (y - \bar{y})^2$$

This expression measures the extent to which y varies from its average value. It uses squares for the same reason that the residuals are squared in the least-squares criterion. Part of this variation can be thought of as being 'caused' by the x variable. This is the purpose of regression and correlation, to investigate the extent to which changes in y are affected by changes in x. The variation in y that is 'caused' by x is called the explained variation. It can be measured from the difference between the fitted y value and the average y value:

$$\text{explained variation} = \text{sum (fitted } y - \bar{y})^2$$

Since the fitted y values are calculated from the regression equation, this variation is understood, hence 'explained'. Another part of the

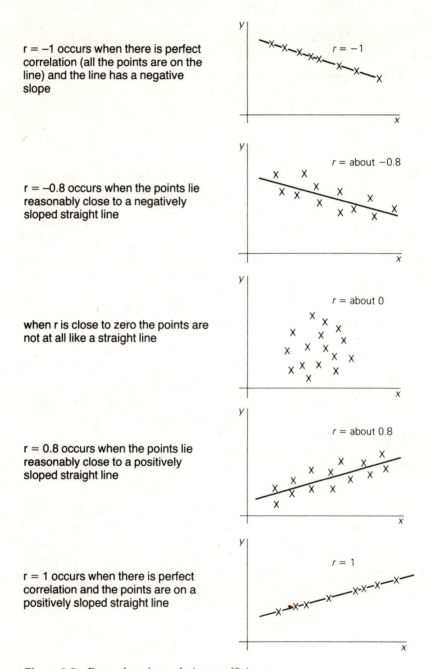

r = −1 occurs when there is perfect correlation (all the points are on the line) and the line has a negative slope

r = −0.8 occurs when the points lie reasonably close to a negatively sloped straight line

when r is close to zero the points are not at all like a straight line

r = 0.8 occurs when the points lie reasonably close to a positively sloped straight line

r = 1 occurs when there is perfect correlation and the points are on a positively sloped straight line

Figure 3.5 Examples of correlation coefficients.

total variation in y is 'unexplained'. This is the variation in the residuals, the 'left-over' variation which is not understood:

$$\text{unexplained variation} = \text{sum (residuals)}^2$$

Note that it is this unexplained variation which least-squares regression minimizes. Using some more 'black box' mathematics, it is possible to show that

$$\text{total variation} = \text{explained variation} + \text{unexplained variation}$$

This fact is used to define the correlation coefficient:

$$R^2 = \frac{\text{explained variation}}{\text{total variation}}$$

This indicates why the correlation coefficient squared works as a measure of the strength of a relationship. If $R^2 = 1$, then

$$\text{explained variation} = \text{total variation}$$

and, $$\text{unexplained variation} = 0$$

If the unexplained variation is equal to zero then the sum of all the residuals is zero and therefore all the residuals must individually be equal to zero. The points must all lie exactly on the line. $R^2 = 1$ thus signifies perfect correlation. If $R^2 = 0$ then

$$\text{unexplained variation} = \text{total variation}$$

The regression line does not explain variations in y in any way. The residuals vary just as much as the bare values of y. The points are not at all like a straight line.

Because variation is measured in squared terms the ratio is labelled R squared (R^2). Sometimes a computer regression program will print out r and sometimes R squared. r has the advantage of distinguishing between positive and negative correlation; R squared has the advantage of a better intuitive meaning. .

To summarize, the essence of correlation is that in carrying out a regression analysis, the variation in the y variable is split into two parts:

1 A part that is 'explained' by virtue of associating the y values with the x.

2 A part that is 'unexplained' since the relationship is not an exact one.

The correlation coefficient squared tells what proportion of the original variation in y has been explained by drawing a line through

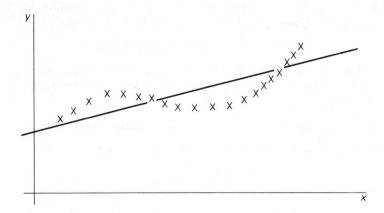

Figure 3.6   Non-random residuals.

the points. The higher the proportion, the stronger the correlation is said to be. Deciding whether, statistically, R^2 is high enough in a particular case requires the use of a complicated test. Rather than using such a test it is more important for a manager to ask a slightly different but related question: are the forecasts accurate enough for the decision they are to support? The basis for answering this question is described in the next section.

Using the Residuals

Once the regression equation has been found the residuals can be calculated as the difference between actual and fitted y values. In the previous regression example, the residuals can be calculated as in table 3.1.

Table 3.1   Calculation of Residuals.

Actual		Fitted	Residual
x	y	y	actual y − fitted y
1	20	18 (= 14 + 4 × 1)	2 (= 20 − 18)
2	19	22 (= 14 + 4 × 2)	−3 (= 19 − 22)
4	34	30 (= 14 + 4 × 4)	4 (= 34 − 30)
5	30	34 (= 14 + 4 × 5)	−4 (= 30 − 34)
8	47	46 (= 14 + 4 × 8)	1 (= 47 − 46)

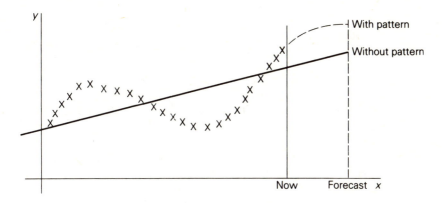

Figure 3.7 The effect of not incorporating a seasonal pattern or cycle.

There are two main reasons why the residuals of a regression analysis are important, apart from their role as the basis of the least squares criterion.

Residuals Should be Random

The correlation coefficient is one test for deciding whether the two variables are linked. By itself, however, this test is not sufficient. A further test is that the residuals should be random; random means without any pattern or order. Figure 3.6 shows a scatter diagram for which the correlation coefficient is high but for which a straight line does not fully represent the way in which the variables are linked. There is another effect, probably a seasonal pattern or cycle, which should be incorporated (in a way as yet unspecified) into the forecast. Figure 3.7 shows how different the forecasts might be if this effect were not incorporated.

The first way of testing for randomness is visual. The scatter diagram, now including the best fit line, is inspected for patterns such as those in figure 3.6. (See figure 3.8.) In figure 3.8 a visual test is all that is necessary to detect the obvious pattern. Other situations are inevitably not so clear-cut. There may be a hint of a pattern but it is not definite. In these circumstances, statistical tests of randomness are a more precise approach to the problem. In practice, visual inspection is usually more than adequate.

There are many statistical tests for randomness. The runs test is a common example. It works in the following way. A 'run' is a group of

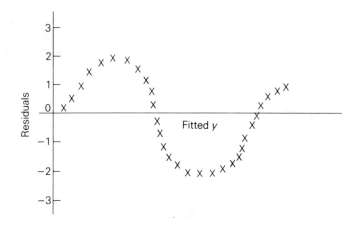

Figure 3.8   Residuals plotted against fitted *y* values.

consecutive residuals with the same sign. As an example, the ten residuals in figure 3.9 have four runs.

Residuals: +3.1, −1.6, −0.2, −1.4, +1.1, +2.9, +0.3, −1.0, −3.1, −0.1
Runs: ←1→←——2——→←——3——→←——4——→

Figure 3.9   Runs.

If the residuals have a small number of runs then they are unlikely to be random. This could arise from a situation like that shown in figure 3.10(a). If the residuals have a large number of runs then again they are unlikely to be random. This could arise from the situation shown in figure 3.10(b).

A runs test is based on an expected number of runs which is the number of runs that would be most likely to occur if the residuals were random. This is compared with the actual number of runs counted in the residuals in question. If the actual differs from the expected by a large margin, the residuals will be assumed to be non-random. The detail of the statistical background to the runs test (how the expected number of runs is calculated and what a significant difference is between actual and expected) are 'black box' matters beyond the scope of this text. The sign test, in which the number of times the residuals change sign is counted, is sometimes used in place of the runs test. The two are exactly equivalent since the number of sign changes must always be one fewer than the number of runs.

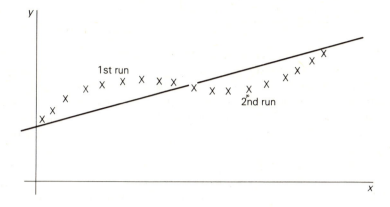

Figure 3.10(a) Residuals with a small number of runs.

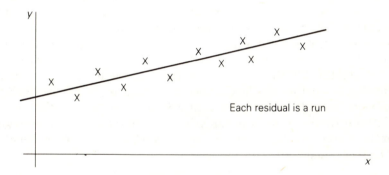

Figure 3.10(b) Residuals with a large number of runs.

Residuals and Forecasting Accuracy

A single forecast for a future moment in time is called a point forecast. How accurate is this likely to be? To a large extent the residuals determine the accuracy of forecasts. Intuitively, this makes sense. The residuals are the historical differences between the actual values and the regression line. It is to be expected that actual values in the future will differ from the regression line by similar amounts. The size of the residuals is therefore an indication of forecasting accuracy.

An overall measure of the size of residuals is their *standard error*. It is based on the sum of residuals squared, which is, of course, the foundation of the least squares criterion. The standard error is a common statistical measure of scatter.

$$\text{Standard error of residuals} = \frac{\text{sum (residuals)}^2}{\text{number of observations}}$$

The standard error of predicted values or standard error (predicted) also measures forecasting accuracy. This measure is slightly larger than the standard error of residuals because it makes additional allowance for inaccuracy in estimating the equation coefficients, a and b. The formula for calculating this quantity is, as might be expected, fairly complicated. Fortunately most computer forecasting packages print it out automatically.

Statistical theory states that provided there are (as a rule of thumb) more than 30 data points, 95 per cent of future values of the variable are likely to lie within +/−2 standard errors (predicted) of the point forecast. This is a forecast interval. It is used to decide whether the level of accuracy is sufficient for the decisions being taken.

For example, suppose an organization is forecasting its profit in the next financial year in order to take pricing decisions. The point forecast is $50 million and the standard error (predicted) is $4 million. Therefore it is 95 per cent probable that the profit will turn out to be in the range $42 million to $58 million (+ or −2 standard errors). Whatever the statistical niceties of the regression model, the real question is whether this level of accuracy is adequate for the pricing decision. Would radically different decisions be taken if the profit were at extreme parts of this range? If so, then the search must go on for more accurate predictions; if not, then what would be the benefit of further refinement of the model?

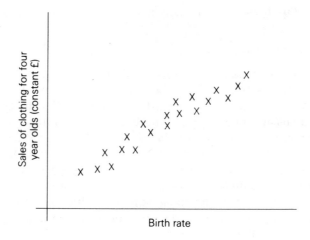

Figure 3.11   A scatter diagram relating clothing sales and birth rate.

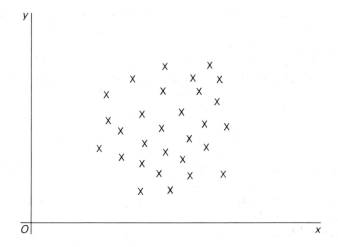

Figure 3.12 A non-linear scatter diagram.

Causal Modelling on a Microcomputer

A retail clothing company is trying to forecast its sales of four-year-old children's clothing as part of its corporate plan. As a first step a causal model relating nationwide sales to the birth rate four years previously is investigated; this makes sense since sales must be related in some way to the number of children needing clothes. Annual data on sales (in constant price terms) and the birth rate for the last 20 years are available on a microcomputer. To make the explanation easier, assume that the variables were labelled 'sales' and 'births' when they were entered into the computer. Making a forecast involves the following steps. (Note that while every statistical package is different, virtually all of them have the capability to carry out the steps. The package manual will show exactly which commands will produce the desired effect.)

Look at the Scatter Diagram

To produce a scatter diagram the computer will ask for a variable to go on the vertical axis and one to go on the horizontal axis. Answer 'sales' and 'births' respectively. Figure 3.11 is a scatter diagram relating the data on clothing sales to the birth rate. There are 20 points on the diagram, one for each of the 20 years. Each point marks off the sales and birth rate in a particular year. The diagram confirms that there is an approximate straight-line relationship between the two variables. It makes sense to consider simple linear regression in this case. Had the diagram looked like figure 3.12, there would have been no evidence of a linear relationship and little reason to proceed further with the analysis. A scatter diagram is a first check that the analysis makes sense. It also gives the analyst better insight and more direct knowledge of the situation.

Carry Out a Regression Analysis

The computer will ask for the dependent variable (the y variable: in this case 'sales') and the independent variable (the x variable: in this case 'births'). The output will vary from package to package but will be similar to the following:

	Coefficient
Births	3.14
Constant	8.65

R squared   0.93
Standard error of residuals 5.62

This output means that the equation relating sales and births is:

$$\text{Sales} = 8.65 + 3.14 \times \text{births}$$

If the births four years ago were 18, then the estimate for sales this year would be:

$$\begin{aligned}\text{Sales} &= 8.65 + 3.14 \times 18 \\ &= 8.65 + 56.52 \\ &= 65.17\end{aligned}$$

R squared is 0.93, indicating a high level of correlation, 93 per cent of the variation in sales being accounted for. This verifies the intuitive conclusion obtained from the scatter diagram.

The residual standard error is 5.62. This figure is less important than the others but it does give an idea of the accuracy of any forecasts made. The '95 per cent probable' range for the sales will be at least as wide as plus or minus twice the residual standard error, i.e. + or −11.24.

Examine the Residuals

Ask the computer to produce a scatter diagram of the residuals against the fitted values. This is shown in figure 3.13. The x-axis, the fitted values, is in effect the regression line. The residuals should be

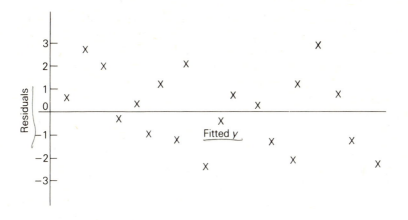

Figure 3.13   A residual scatter diagram.

random. If there is a pattern in them it should be evident in the movement of the residuals around the *x*-axis. A pattern might be a cyclical variation (figure 3.14(a)) or a tendency for residuals to vary in size at different parts of the line (figure 3.14(b)). If there is a pattern, a visual test with a scatter diagram is usually sufficient to detect it. However, at this point it is possible to use statistical tests for randomness which are available on most software packages. Many such tests exist. Any one package will not offer them all. The runs test described on p. 43 is frequently offered.

When a runs test is called for, the computer prints out the actual number of runs counted in the residuals in question; it prints out an expected number of runs, which is the number of runs that would be most likely to occur if the residuals were random; it also prints out a range either side of this expected number. The range is the area into which the actual number of runs should fall if, statistically speaking, the residuals can be said to be random. If the actual number of runs does fall within the range then the residuals are assumed to be random, otherwise not.

In this case of sales forecasting, the computer prints out the following:

> Actual number of runs   6
> Expected number of runs   5
> 95 per cent range for expected number of runs 2.2–7.8

Since the number of runs falls within the range the conclusion is that the residuals are random.

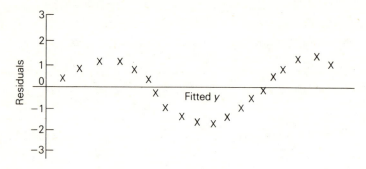

Figure 3.14(a)   Cyclical variation of residuals.

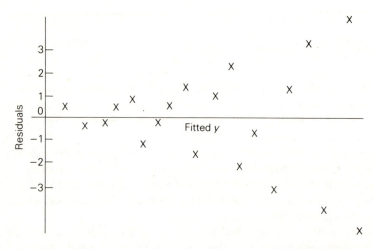

Figure 3.14(b)   Residuals varying in size at different parts of the line.

Make Predictions

The computer will not make predictions as a matter of course. It may be that the regression analysis or residuals were in some way unsatisfactory and a new model has to be researched. However, if the model has proved satisfactory the package can be commanded to make predictions. It will ask for the value of the independent variable (18 births in this case) to which the prediction relates and then print out:

                    Births   18.00
                    Estimated sales   65.17
                    Standard error (predicted)   7.12

The point estimate for sales is 65.17. The 95 per cent probable forecast interval is + or − 2 × 7.12, i.e. the range is 50.93 to 79.41. Note that the standard error (predicted) is larger than the standard error of the residuals since the former makes allowance for errors in estimating the coefficient of births (3.14) as well as allowing for errors resulting from the residuals.

Most computer packages are sufficiently flexible to carry out sophisticated analyses. Unfortunately this means that their output is also sophisticated. The output shown above is the bare minimum. In most cases it is difficult to find the required estimates and statistics from the profusion which is produced.

Multiple Regression Analysis

The regression analysis so far has been simple regression. The dependent variable 'sales' has been related to the one independent variable 'births'. It is fairly obvious, however, that there must be factors other than births influencing sales. For instance, the amount of money in the national economy must have an effect on the volume of children's clothes bought. How can this and other influences be incorporated into the forecasts of sales? The answer is to use multiple regression analysis.

In simple regression the equation is of the form:

$$y = a + bx$$

In multiple regression the basic idea is extended to two or more variables on the right-hand side of the equation. For example, using three x variables:

$$y = a + bx + cz + dt$$

There are three independent variables x, z, t; their coefficients are b, c, d; the constant is a. The criterion for multiple regression is the same as for simple: the sum of squared residuals is to be minimized. Inevitably the formulae for calculating a, b, c, d are more complicated but this makes little difference if a computer is being used.

In the sales example, suppose a second independent variable is to be included to reflect the influence of the economic environment. Gross domestic product (GDP) is often used in this role. The procedure is very much the same as in simple regression.

1 *Inspect the scatter diagrams* to see whether approximate relationships

do exist. This time there will be two diagrams: sales/births and sales/GDP.

2 *Carry out the regression.* The computer will ask for the name of the dependent variable, then those of the independent variables. The printout will read:

	Coefficient
Births	2.23
GDP	0.35
Constant	4.28
R squared 0.97	
Residual standard error 3.87	

The equation predicting sales is now:

$$\text{Sales} = 4.28 + 2.23 \times \text{births} + 0.35 \times \text{GDP}$$

Notice that the coefficient for births is now 2.23, whereas for simple regression it was 3.14. The addition of an extra variable changes the previous coefficients, including the constant.

R squared has risen to 0.97. The presence of GDP has therefore increased the proportion of variation explained. Similarly the residual standard error has decreased. In other words the residuals are, generally, smaller.

3 *Examine the residuals.* This is exactly the same as for simple regression. A scatter diagram of residuals against fitted values is inspected for randomness. A runs test is still applicable.

4 *Make predictions.* Again the procedure is the same, except that a value for GDP as well as births will be requested in order to make the prediction. A point estimate of sales will be printed out together with the standard error (predicted) which is interpreted just as before.

This outline of the main principles of multiple regression inevitably masks some of the statistical detail. For example, in many situations there is a long list of candidates for inclusion as independent variables. How should the decision be made to include some and leave out others? Common sense and the conceptual model (in the checklist of chapter 1) is the basic method of deciding which to try. However, there are also statistical procedures to help with this problem. They depend upon the statistical theory of regression analysis.

The Statistical Basis of Regression and Correlation

To start, the discussion will be restricted to simple linear regression. If it is believed that the two variables are linearly related, then the statistician hypothesizes that, in the full set of all possible observations on the two variables (known as the population), a straight-line relationship does exist. Any deviations from this (in effect, the residuals) are caused by minor random disturbances, such as, for example, measurement errors. A sample is then taken from the population and used to estimate the equation's coefficients, the correlation coefficient and other statistics. This sample is merely the set of points upon which calculations of a, b and r have been based up to now.

However, the fact that these calculations are made from sample data means that a, b and r are no more than estimates. Had a different sample been chosen, different values would have been obtained. Were it possible to take many samples, distributions of the coefficients would be obtained. In practice, only one sample need be taken since the distributions can be estimated from it. In effect, the variation of the distribution is estimated from the variations in the residuals resulting from the one sample.

These distributions (of a, b, r and other statistics) are the basis of statistical tests of whether the hypothesis of a straight-line relationship in the population is true. They are also the basis for determining the accuracy of regression predictions. In particular, the statistical approach is the means for deciding how many and which independent variables to keep in the regression equation.

The statistical approach to regression analysis enables a *significance test* to be carried out for each variable. The test works as follows. Use the hypothesis that the particular variable has no effect on the y variable, or, in other words, that the true coefficient of the variable, as measured from the population, is zero. The distribution (discussed above) of estimates of this coefficient should then be centred on zero. The estimate of the coefficient obtained from the regression may be small or large but it is unlikely to be exactly zero, except by a fluke. Two interpretations could be put on this non-zero coefficient:

1 Although non-zero, the coefficient is nevertheless consistent with a distribution centred on zero. A non-zero value has arisen purely by chance. It does not contradict the hypothesis that the true coefficient is zero.

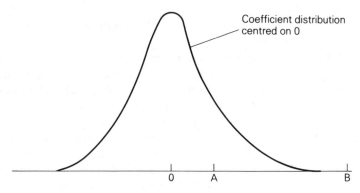

Figure 3.15   A zero-centred distribution.

2 The coefficient is not consistent with a zero-centred distribution. It is sufficiently far from zero to lie outside (or at an extreme of) the distribution. The regression result contradicts the hypothesis that the true coefficient is zero.

Which of these interpretations should be accepted depends upon the size of the estimated coefficient compared to the spread (or width) of the distribution. These two factors govern whether the estimate is consistent with (i.e. falls within) the zero-centred distribution or not. In figure 3.15 a coefficient estimate at point A is consistent with the distribution. The hypothesis, that the true coefficient is zero, would therefore be accepted. The variable has no effect in the regression equation and can be discarded. A coefficient at point B is not consistent with a zero-centred distribution. The hypothesis would be rejected and the variable retained in the regression equation.

In practice, the decision to accept or reject the hypothesis (respectively, to discard or keep the variable) is based on the *t* value which is the ratio between the coefficient estimate and the standard error of the distribution. As before, standard error is a measure of spread. In this case it relates to the width of the coefficient's distribution. The larger the *t* value, the further the estimate is from the middle of the zero-centred distribution. The *t* value is usually given automatically as part of the computer output. As a rule of thumb, if it exceeds 2 (or is less than −2), the variable should be retained; if it lies between −2 and +2, the variable should be discarded. The statistical theory underlying the *t* value will not be discussed but its calculation (coefficient/standard error) can be verified from most printouts.

Example. An earlier example was concerned with predicting the sales of clothing for four-year-old children by relating it to the number of births four years earlier and the gross domestic product (GDP). A third variable, the store's advertising expenditure that year, is added to the equation. The computer output for this multiple regression is shown in table 3.2. Are all the three variables: births, GDP and advertising rightfully included in the regression equation?

Table 3.2 Multiple regression

Variable	Coefficient	Standard error	*t* value
Births	2.07	0.35	5.9
GDP	0.28	0.11	2.5
Advertising	6.12	4.80	1.3
Constant	2.86		
R squared = 0.98			
Residual standard error = 2.34			

[handwritten annotations:] this no t = signifi cant variable because its less than 2 (T<2). + more than -2 (2<T<2) ie range (2<T<2) not signif continuous

The computer output given above is more extensive than any shown up to now. This output includes the coefficient standard errors and *t* values. Most packages would show at least this much information. Verify that the *t* values are the ratio between the coefficient estimate and the standard error.

To answer the question, one has only to look to see which *t* values are inside the range −2 to +2. For births and GDP the *t* values, at 5.9 and 2.5, exceed 2. Both these variables therefore have a significant effect on the sales of clothing and are rightfully included in the equation. The *t* value for advertising is 1.3, less than 2. According to the statistical test, advertising does not have a significant effect on clothing sales. The variable can be eliminated from the equation.

The aim of this section has been to present the principles behind the procedure for deciding which variables to include in a regression equation. In using the procedure you need to be cautious. First, only the outlines of the statistical theory have been described. There are circumstances in which the procedure should be modified. In particular, the 'critical' *t* value of 2 is just a rule of thumb. For small samples (fewer than 30 observations) that value depends upon the size of the sample. The second note of caution is that this procedure is a purely statistical one and should not be applied too slavishly. For instance, in the example above the negative information from the *t* value should be balanced against wider knowledge that perhaps, advertising really does have an effect on sales. It may be valid to put aside the statistical results in some situations. The procedure is an important guide, but no more, as to which variables to include.

Some Reservations about Regression and Correlation

Causality is probably the largest single source of confusion and error. Carrying out regression analysis on a microcomputer deals with the statistical aspects of a relationship. Potentially more important are the interpretive aspects. Even when a relationship passes all the statistical tests, what can be concluded and how can the results be used?

It is essential to remember that while the statistics can show whether the variables are associated, they do not say that changes in one variable cause changes in another. Some examples will illustrate the point.

There is alleged to be a close association (indicated by high correlation, random residuals etc.) between the price of rum and the remuneration of the clergy. This does not mean that the two variables are causally related. A rise in salary for the clergy will not, presumably, be spent on rum, thereby depleting stocks and causing a rise in price. It is more likely that there is a third factor, such as inflation or the general level of society's affluence, which affects both variables so that in the past the salaries and the price of rum have moved together. It would be a mistake to suppose that, if conditions were to change, the relationship must continue to hold. If, for some philanthropic purpose, the clergy agreed to take a cut in salary one year, it is unlikely that the price of rum would fall as well. The price of rum would continue to change in response to inflation or whatever. Different circumstances now apply to clergy salaries and the association is broken.

The point is that a causal relationship will hold through changing circumstances (provided the causal link is not broken); a purely associative relationship is likely to be broken as circumstances change. The application to forecasting is clear. If the relationship is associative, beware of changing circumstances.

The difference between a causal and an associative relationship depends upon its structure, not upon the statistics. Common sense and logic are the ways to distinguish between the two. In the case of rum and the clergy, no-one would seriously argue that the link is causal; in the case of sales of four-year-old children's clothing and births four years earlier there is some sort of causal link (although of course there are other influences operating).

Spurious regressions should be guarded against. Spurious means that the correlation coefficient is high but there is no underlying relationship. This may arise purely by chance when the sample of observations used in the analysis just happen to have a high correlation. If other observations were taken, no correlation would be apparent.

Spurious correlations may also arise because of a fault in the regression model. For example, a study sought to determine the relationship between the profitability of companies and their size. Profitability was measured by return on net assets; size was measured by net profit. The equation was:

$$\text{return on net assets} = a + b \times \text{net profit}$$

The observations were taken from a sample of companies. Such a regression has an in-built likelihood of a high correlation since:

$$\text{return on net assets} = \frac{\text{net profit}}{\text{net assets}}$$

The regression equation is:

$$\text{net profit/net assets} = a + b \times \text{net profit}$$

Net profit appears in both the y and x variables. If there are only small variations in net assets from company to company, then the tendency will be for high y values to be associated with high x values (and low with low) just because net profit dominates both sides of the equation. A high correlation coefficient would probably result, but it could not be concluded that profitability and size were linked.

Extrapolation should be avoided, if possible. Extrapolation means using the equation outside the range of the data on which the regression was based. For example, if a regression were based on x values in the range 100 to 200, then forecasting the y value for $x = 400$ is extrapolation. This is dangerous because the model is based on x between 100 and 200. Nothing is known about the behaviour of y and x when $x = 400$. Often in forecasting, extrapolation cannot be avoided, but it should be done with caution.

Data which are two separate sets of observations should be avoided. The data in figure 3.16(a) may have a high correlation coefficient, hiding the fact that two separate straight lines (figure 3.16(b)) would be more

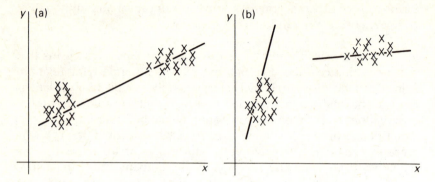

Figure 3.16   Avoid using two sets of observations for correlation. Two lines (b) may be more appropriate than one (a).

appropriate. This highlights the need to be familiar with the data and especially to look at the scatter diagram.

Over-precision can be misleading. The least squares criterion can seem more precise than it is. The three lines A, B and C in figure 3.17 may be very close to one another in terms of variation explained (perhaps less than 1 per cent different), although their equations are very different. The least-squares principle picks out one equation as best, giving the impression that it is clearly the best when other equations may, for all practical purposes, be just as good. They may even be better when non-statistical factors are considered. Prior knowledge or previous work may be more relevant in deciding between A, B and C.

Check for collinearity. What would happen if the same x variable were included twice in the regression equation? In other words, suppose that in the equation below z and t were the same.

$$y = a + bx + cz + dt$$

The answer is that the computer package would be unable to complete the calculations. However, if z and t were almost but not quite the same then the regression could proceed and c and d would be estimated. Clearly, these estimates would have little value; nor would it be easy to determine which of the variables had the greater influence on the y variable.

This, in simple form, is the problem of collinearity (sometimes referred to as multi-collinearity). It occurs when two (or more) of the x variables are highly correlated with one another. In these circumstances

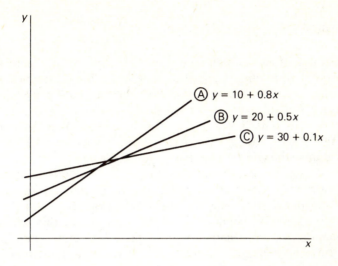

Figure 3.17 Alternative equations.

the two variables are contributing essentially the same information to the regression analysis. Their coefficient estimates are unreliable in the sense that small changes in the observations can produce large changes in the estimates. Regression finds it difficult to discriminate between the effects of the two variables. While the overall equation may still be used for predictions, it cannot be used for assessing the individual effects of the two variables.

The test for collinearity is to inspect the correlation coefficients of all x variables taken in pairs. If any of the coefficients are high, the corresponding two variables are collinear.

There are three remedies for the problem:

1 Use only one of the variables (which to exclude is largely a subjective decision).
2 Amalgamate the variables (say, by adding them together if the amalgamated variable has meaning).
3 Substitute one of the variables with a new variable which has similar meaning but which has a low correlation with the remaining one of the pair.

The test and remedy for collinearity are not precise. It is more important to be aware of the problem and the restrictions it places on interpretation than to delve into the technicalities behind it.

Conclusion

Regression and correlation are important forecasting techniques. They have a wide range of applications, including economics, sales, budgeting, costs, manpower planning and corporate planning. The underlying statistical theory is extensive. Unfortunately, the depth of the subject can in itself lead to errors as forecasters allow the statistics to dominate their thought processes. Many major errors have been made because the wider issues have been neglected.

As well as providing financial expertise, the manager has a role to play in drawing attention to these issues. He should be the one asking the penetrating but non-statistical questions about the way causal modelling is being applied. He cannot do this unless he understands the basic statistical principles. It is only when he has taken the trouble to equip himself in this way that he will be taken seriously when he participates in discussions. Moreover, his own confidence will probably be high enough to participate in the discussions only when he feels relatively at ease with the technicalities. This chapter is intended to provide the necessary statistical equipment for causal modelling. In addition, the chapter has described the major non-statistical considerations – the basis of those penetrating questions. Much of the statistics may appear complicated but it is worth pursuing since the manager's contribution to forecasting is potentially very large.

CHAPTER 4

Time Series Methods

Time series methods are forecasting techniques which predict future values of a variable solely from its own historical record. In various ways they identify patterns in past data and project them into the future. The methods are categorized according to the types of series to which they can be applied. The different types of series are:

Stationary (roughly, without a trend)
With a trend (a consistent movement upwards or downwards)
With a trend and seasonality (a regular pattern that repeats itself every year)
With a trend, seasonality and cycle (a regular pattern that takes more than a year to repeat itself)

This chapter will describe some of the techniques which can deal with these types of data. First, the particular situations in which time series techniques have shown themselves to be successful will be discussed.

Where Time Series Methods Are Successful

At first glance it may seem that such inward-looking techniques are bound to be inferior to both qualitative techniques and causal modelling. When conditions change, time series methods, looking only at the past record, have no way of predicting the change or even responding quickly to it. Nevertheless, there are distinct areas in which they are very successful. When tested, they have compared favourably with the competition, especially in the following circumstances.

In stable conditions. If there are no changing circumstances, it can reasonably be assumed that the factors which caused movements of the variable in the past will continue into the future. Consequently, the time series approach is likely to provide good forecasts.

For short-term forecasts. If there is not sufficient time for any substantial changes in conditions, then time series methods are valid. In the short term most data series continue as in the past.

As a base forecast. The base forecast shows what would be expected if the future were similar to the past. Even when conditions are changing, time series methods provide starting forecasts on which judgements about changing conditions can be built.

For screening data. Time series techniques identify patterns in the historical record. The patterns can be used to obtain a better understanding of past movements. For instance, it might emerge that a particularly high level of sales one month was merely the coincidence of high points in a cycle and in seasonality.

Time series methods have a good record in all the above situations. Surveys of forecasting performance (see Further Reading, p. 194) have frequently shown them to out-perform other approaches. The techniques will now be described. They are categorized according to the series to which they can be applied.

Stationary Series

A data series is stationary if it fluctuates about some constant level and if, while the amount of fluctuation differs from one time period to the next, there is no general tendency for there to be more fluctuation at one part of the series than at another. More technically, a stationary series has no trend and has constant variance.

In the long run, virtually no series are stationary, but they may be in the short run. For example, the weekly stock volumes in a warehouse over two years is a long series (104 observations) which may well be stationary. Over five years it would probably not be.

Two techniques which deal with stationary series will be described, moving averages and exponential smoothing.

Moving Averages

The original series is replaced by a 'smoothed' series, obtained by replacing each actual observation with the average of it and other observations either side of it. If each average is calculated from three actual observations, it is said to be a three-point moving average; if each is calculated from five actual observations, it is a five-point moving average and so on. Table 4.1 gives an example of a three-point moving average.

Table 4.1   A three-point moving average

Time period (t)	Actual series (x)	Smoothed series
1	17	
2	23	17.3 = (17 + 23 + 12)/3
3	12	16.3 = (23 + 12 + 14)/3
4	14	17.3 = (12 + 14 + 26)/3
5	26	18.7 = (14 + 26 + 16)/3
6	16	

Smooth value at time period t =
(actual value at $t - 1$ + actual value at t + actual value at $t + 1$)/3

Algebraically, $S_t = \dfrac{x_{t-1} + x_t + x_{t+1}}{3}$

To help the explanation, some algebra has been introduced. Each number in a data series is given a label, x_t where t refers to the time period. Table 4.2 shows how the labelling works for a quarterly data series from quarter 3, 1981 through 1982.

Table 4.2   Algebraic labelling for a quarterly data series, 1981–2

	1981		1982			
Time period	Q3	Q4	Q1	Q2	Q3	Q4
Data	17	23	12	14	26	16
t	1	2	3	4	5	6
Label	x_1	x_2	x_3	x_4	x_5	x_6

The averaging process is intended to smooth away the random fluctuations in the series. The forecast for any time period is the most recent smoothed value. In the above series, the forecast is 18.7 for all periods in the future. A constant makes sense because the series is stationary.

Seasonal as well as random fluctuations in the data can be smoothed away by including sufficient points in the average to cover the seasonality. Seasonal monthly data would be smoothed using a 12-point moving average. Each month is included once and only once in the average and thus seasonal variation will be averaged out.

The use of an even number of points in a moving average creates a problem. A smoothed value can no longer refer to a particular time period. It must refer to half way between the middle two time periods. For example, a three-point moving average for the months January, February and March is the smooth value for February. A four-point moving average for January, February, March and April is the smooth value for in between February and March. This makes no difference when forecasting a stationary series, but it does have an effect in other uses of moving averages. There will be more on this later.

The number of points included in the moving average is usually equal to the number of seasonal divisions of the data. In the absence of seasonality the average should include sufficient points to be able to smooth the fluctuations, but not so many that the last smoothed value refers to a time period remote from the time periods for which the forecasts are being made. In practice, three- or five-point moving averages are probably the most common.

Even when the data are non-stationary, the method of moving averages can still be used to smooth out random fluctuations, enabling trends and other patterns to be seen more clearly.

Exponential Smoothing

For a moving average, each value in the average is given an equal weight. In a three-point moving average, each value is given a weight of one third. Exponential smoothing is a way of constructing an 'average' which gives more weight to recent values of the variable.

The smoothed series is given by the equation:

new smoothed value
$$= (1 - \alpha) \text{ (previous smoothed value)} + \alpha \text{ (most recent actual value)}$$

i.e., $S_t = (1 - \alpha) . S_{t-1} + \alpha x_t$
where α is between zero and 1

The value of α is chosen by the forecaster. The larger its value, the heavier the weighting being given to the recent values. Its value may be selected after testing out several values and measuring which is the best. In practice a is usually in the range 0.1 to 0.4.

Chapter 6 describes how to compare the effectiveness of different forecasting methods. This can be the basis for choosing a value of a. Exponential smoothing is carried out using different a values and the results compared as if they came from different forecasting methods. The a value giving the best results is chosen for the forecasting proper. An example of this procedure is given in the case study in chapter 9 (p. 159).

Example. The data used in table 4.1 are exponentially smoothed in table 4.3. Since the smoothing equation requires a previous smoothed value to get it started, it is usual to make the first smoothed value equal to the actual value. This assumption will have a negligible effect unless the series is a very short one.

Table 4.3   Exponential smoothing of the data in table 4.1

Original series	Smoothed series (using $\alpha = 0.2$)
17	17
23	18.2 $(= 0.8 \times 17 + 0.2 \times 23)$
12	16.96 $(= 0.8 \times 18.2 + 0.2 \times 12)$
14	16.37 $(= 0.8 \times 16.96 + 0.2 \times 14)$
26	18.30 $(= 0.8 \times 16.37 + 0.2 \times 26)$
16	17.84 $(= 0.8 \times 18.30 + 0.2 \times 16)$

Figure 4.1 shows how exponential smoothing works to average out random fluctuations. As with moving averages, the forecast for future time periods of a stationary series is the most recent smoothed value, in this case 17.84.

Technical note. A little algebraic manipulation is required to show why exponential smoothing gives different weighting to different time periods. The equation for exponential smoothing is:

$$S_t = (1 - a) \cdot S_{t-1} + ax_t$$

But, from the previous time period:

$$S_{t-1} = (1 - a) \cdot S_{t-2} + ax_{t-1}$$

Putting this S_{t-1} in the top equation gives

$$S_t = (1 - a)^2 \cdot S_{t-2} + (1 - a) ax_{t-1} + ax_t$$

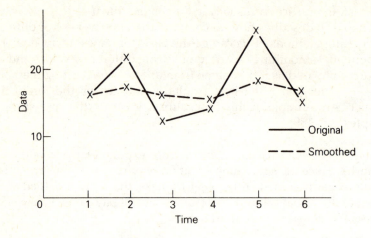

Figure 4.1 Exponential smoothing.

Just as S_{t-1} in the original equation was substituted, so S_{t-2} can be substituted. Continuing this process eventually gives:

$$S_t = \alpha x_t + \alpha(1-\alpha)x_{t-1} + \alpha(1-\alpha)^2 x_{t-2} + \alpha(1-\alpha)^3 x_{t-3} + \ldots$$

The weightings being given to past values are:

$$\alpha,\ \alpha(1-\alpha),\ \alpha(1-\alpha)^2,\ \alpha(1-\alpha)^3 \ldots$$

Since α, and thus $1-\alpha$, lie between zero and 1, these weightings are decreasing. For instance if $\alpha = 0.2$, the weightings are:

$$0.2, 0.16, 0.128, 0.1024, 0.0819, \ldots$$

Recent actual values receive heavier weighting than earlier ones. The smoothing equation derived above illustrates how the weighting works. It is not intended to be used for calculations.

Series with a Trend

The use of moving averages or exponential smoothing may reveal the existence of a trend. Or the trend may have been immediately obvious without any smoothing. For a non-stationary series these two techniques have to be adapted before they can be used. There are several variants of moving averages and exponential smoothing that can deal with a trend. The one described here is Holt's method, which is a form of exponential smoothing.

Holt's Method

The formula for exponential smoothing is:

$$S_t = (1 - a) . S_{t-1} + ax_t$$

If the series has a trend the smoothed value S_t (which is the forecast for future time periods) will generally be too low since (a) it is formed in part from the previous smoothed value S_{t-1} and (b) the forecast does not allow for the effect of a trend on future values. If there is a trend, it should be seen in the smoothed values; therefore a first way of calculating a trend might be:

trend = most recent smoothed value – previous smoothed value
i.e., trend at time $t = S_t - S_{t-1}$

Just as random fluctuations in the actual data can be smoothed, so it is with the trend. A smoothed estimate of the trend is obtained by using a smoothing constant (labelled γ) to combine the most recently observed trends $(S_t - S_{t-1})$ with the previous smoothed trend. γ is between zero and 1, is chosen by the forecaster and may or may not be different from a.

Smoothed trend = $(1-\gamma)$. previous smoothed trend
  $+ \gamma$. most recently observed trend
i.e., $b_t = (1 - \gamma) . b_{t-1} + \gamma . (S_t - S_{t-1})$

How is this estimate of the trend used in conjunction with the exponential smoothing formula? Firstly, the basic formula is changed so that the previous smoothed value, S_{t-1}, is increased to allow for the trend.

$$S_t = (1 - a) S_{t-1} + ax_t$$
becomes:
$$S_t = (1 - a) (S_{t-1} + b_{t-1}) + ax_t$$

Secondly, future forecast values allow for the effect of the trend. A forecast for three periods ahead is no longer S_t, but:

forecast three periods ahead = most recent smoothed value
  $+3 \times$ trend

More generally, the forecast for n periods ahead, F_{t+m} is given by:

$$F_{t+m} = S_t + m.b_t$$

To summarize, when a time series has a trend, forecasts with Holt's method are based on three equations:

$$S_t = (1 - \alpha) . (S_{t-1} + b_{t-1}) + \alpha x_t$$
$$b_t = (1 - \gamma) b_{t-1} + \gamma (S_t - S_{t-1})$$
$$F_{t+m} = S_t + m . b_t$$

where
x_t = actual observation at time t
S_t = smoothed value at time t
α, γ = smoothing constants between zero and 1
b_t = smoothed trend at time t
F_{t+m} = forecast for m periods ahead

Table 4.4 shows how Holt's method is applied to an annual series of sales figures. The series has been shortened in order to simplify the example. The smoothing constants have values:

$$\alpha = 0.2$$
$$\gamma = 0.3$$

The choice of smoothing constants is based on the same principles as for ordinary exponential smoothing.

The calculating process needs a starting point both for the trend and for the smoothed values. The smoothed values for the first two time periods are taken to be equal to the actual values. There can be no trend for the first time period. The smoothed trend for the second time period is taken to be equal to the difference between the first two actual values.

Table 4.4   Holt's method applied to an annual series of sales figures

Year	Sales volume	$\alpha = 0.2$ Smoothing sales	$\gamma = 0.3$ Smoothed trend
(t)	(x_t)	(s_t)	(b_t)
1975	12	12.0	—
1976	15	15.0	3.00
1977	20	$18.4 = 0.8(15.0 + 3.0) + 0.2 \times 20$	$3.12 = 0.7(3.00) + 0.3(18.4 - 15.0)$
1978	21	$21.4 = 0.8(18.4 + 3.12) + 0.2 \times 21$	$3.08 = 0.7(3.12) + 0.3(21.4 - 18.4)$
1979	25	$24.6 = 0.8(21.4 + 3.08) + 0.2 \times 25$	$3.12 = 0.7(3.08) + 0.3(24.6 - 21.4)$
1980	28	$27.8 = 0.8(24.6 + 3.12) + 0.2 \times 28$	$3.14 = 0.7(3.12) + 0.3(27.8 - 24.6)$
	Forecasts		
1981		$30.94 = 27.8 + 3.14$	
1982		$34.08 = 27.8 + 2 \times 3.14$	
1983		$37.22 = 27.8 + 3 \times 3.14$	

Series with a Trend and Seasonality

Seasonality is defined as some regular pattern of upward and downward movements which repeats itself every year or less. There are several techniques which can deal with a series with trend and seasonality. The one described here is the Holt–Winters method which is an extension of Holt's method.

Holt–Winters Method

The Holt's method formulae are:

$$S_t = (1 - \alpha) . (S_{t-1} + b_{t-1}) + \alpha . x_t$$
$$b_t = (1 - \gamma) . b_{t-1} + \gamma (S_t - S_{t-1})$$

The seasonality in a series is seen in that some time periods (months, quarters etc.) are always above or below the smoothed value. It is therefore measured as the ratio between actual and smoothed values. For any time period:

$$seasonality = \frac{x_t}{S_t}$$

Just as the trend was smoothed in the Holt method, so is the seasonality here. Naturally, a further smoothing constant, β, is required.

Smoothed seasonality = $(1 - \beta)$. (previous smoothed seasonality for this time period)
  + β (most recently observed seasonality)

$$I_t = (1 - \beta) . I_{t-12} + \beta . \frac{x_t}{S_t}$$

The above equation refers to a monthly seasonal pattern. If the calculation is being made for, say, January, then the previous smoothed seasonality refers to the previous January, 12 periods ago. Hence the presence of I_{t-12} in the equation.

The complete system of equations for the Holt–Winters method is:

$$S_t = (1 - \alpha) (S_{t-1} + b_{t-1}) + \alpha . \frac{x_t}{I_{t-12}} \quad \text{Smoothed original series}$$

$$b_t = (1 - \gamma) b_{t-1} + \gamma (S_t - S_{t-1}) \qquad \text{Smoothing trend}$$

$$I_t = (1 - \beta) I_{t-12} + \beta . \frac{x_t}{S_t} \qquad \text{Smoothing seasonality}$$

$$F_{t+m} = (S_t + m . b_t) I_{t+m-12} \qquad \text{Forecasting}$$

In smoothing the original series, allowance is made for the seasonality, which is removed from the actual values by dividing by the seasonal effect.

The trend equation is exactly the same as for the Holt method. Forecasting with Holt–Winters takes the latest smoothed value, adds a trend allowance and then multiplies by the seasonal effect. Table 4.5 shows the application of Holt–Winters to a quarterly data series. One of the difficulties in using Holt–Winters on a short series such as this, is that the starting assumptions have an untoward effect. There are refinements to the method which go some way to overcoming this problem. Note that α, β, γ have been given relatively large values so

Table 4.5   The Holt–Winters method applied to a quarterly data series

Year	Quarter	Sales	$\alpha = 0.4$ Smoothed	$\gamma = 0.3$ Trend	$\beta = 0.2$ Seasonality
1980	1	25	25.0	—	—
	2	28	28.0	3.0	—
	3	33	31.8	3.2	—
	4	25	31.0	2.0	—
1981	1	27	30.6	1.3	0.88
	2	36	33.6	1.8	1.07
	3	41	37.6	2.5	1.09
	4	29	35.6	1.1	0.81
1982	1	32	36.6	1.1	0.88
	2	40	37.5	1.0	1.07
	3	46	40.0	1.5	1.10
	4	32	40.6	1.2	0.81
1983	1	35	41.0	1.0	0.87
	2	44	41.6	0.9	1.07
	3	51	44.0	1.3	1.11
	4	37	45.5	1.4	0.81
			Forecasts		
1984	1		40.8 (= (45.5 + 1.4) × 0.87)		
	2		51.6		
	3		55.1		
	4		41.3		

that the system adapts quickly and the influence of the starting assumptions diminishes rapidly.

Series with a Trend, Seasonality and Cycles

A cycle is a regular repeating pattern of upward and downward movements greater than one year in length. Contrast this with seasonality in which the patterns repeat in no more than a year. One of the most common methods of dealing with the three elements – trend, seasonality and cycle – is the charmingly titled decomposition method.

Decomposition Method

The method is based on the supposition that a time series can be separated or decomposed into four distinct elements:

Trend

Cycle

Seasonality

Random

The first three of these elements are then reassembled to make a forecast.

The elements are isolated one by one.

Trend. The trend is isolated by regression analysis between the data and time (see figure 4.2), i.e. the observations (x_t) are regressed against time (t) where t takes on the value 1 for the first time period, 2 for the second, 3 for the third . . . The regression equation will be:

$$x_t = \qquad a + b \cdot t + \qquad u_t$$

actual data	trend element	residuals comprising seasonality, cycles random element

Cycles. The next step is to isolate any cycle in the data. By choosing a suitable moving average (12 points for monthly data, four for quarterly etc.) the random and seasonal elements can be smoothed away, leaving just the trend and cycle. If S_t is such a moving average then

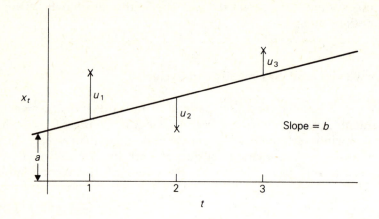

Figure 4.2   Regression analysis between data and time.

the ratio between S_t and the trend $(a + bt)$ must be the cycle. If the ratio $S_t/(a + bt)$ is approximately 1 for all time periods then there is no cycle. If it differs from 1 with any regular pattern then the ratio should be inspected to determine the nature of the cycle. For instance, if the ratio is graphed against time, it might appear as in figure 4.3. This suggests a cycle of period 12 quarters, or three years. The ratio returns to its starting point after this interval of time. The size of the cyclical effect is measured by calculating the average of the ratio for each point in the cycle. For example, for the fifth time period in the cycle $(t = 5, 17, 29 \ldots)$:

$$\text{cyclical effect} = \text{average of } \frac{S_5}{a + 5b}, \ \frac{S_{17}}{a + 17b}, \ \frac{S_{29}}{a + 29b} \quad \cdots$$
$$\text{for } t = 5, 17, 29 \ldots$$

Seasonality. Seasonality is isolated by an approach similar to that used for cycles. The moving agerage, S_t, comprises trend and cycle; the actual values comprise trend, cycle, seasonality and random effect. The ratio:

$$\frac{\text{actual values}}{\text{moving average}} \quad \text{or,} \quad \frac{x_t}{S_t}$$

should therefore reflect seasonality and random effect. Suppose the data are quarterly, then the seasonality for, say, the first quarter is calculated by averaging the ratios:

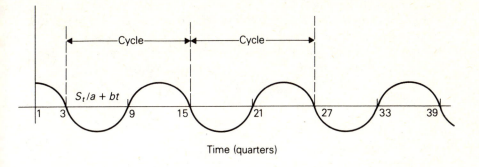

Figure 4.3 at top of page shows curve labeled $S_t/a + bt$ with Cycle brackets and time axis marked 1 3 9 15 21 27 33 39.

Figure 4.3 The ratio $S_t/(a + bt)$ graphed against time.

$$\text{seasonality for first quarter} = \text{average of } \frac{x_1}{S_1}, \frac{x_5}{S_5}, \frac{x_9}{S_9} \cdots$$

The seasonality for the other three quarters can be calculated similarly. The averaging helps to eliminate the random effect which is contained in the ratios.

In making a forecast, the three isolated elements are multiplied together. Suppose the forecast for a future quarter, $t = 50$, is needed. It will be calculated:

forecast $=$ trend $\times$ cycle $\times$ seasonality for $t = 50$

If the data are quartely with a cycle of length 12 quarters, $t = 50$ is the second period of a cycle and the second period of the seasonality. Therefore:

forecast $= (a + 50b) \times$ cyclical effect for second period of the cycle $\times$ seasonal effect for second quarter

·*Example*. The data in table 4.6 are the quarterly shipments of an electrical product from a company's warehouse. Make a forecast of elements in each quarter of 1983 using the decomposition method.

1 Calculate the trend. A regression analysis is carried out with the shipments as the y variable and time as the x variable:

$$y \quad 4.8 \ 6.9 \ 5.9 \ 8.1 \ 6.6 \ 9.5 \ \cdots$$
$$x \quad 1 \quad 2 \quad 3 \quad 4 \quad 5 \quad 6 \ \cdots$$

The analysis gives: shipments $= 2.851 + 0.838 \times$ time.

2 Calculate the cyclical effect. This effect is calculated as the ratio between a moving average and the trend. The moving average has to be a four-point average to include each of the quarters in every average and thus smooth out seasonality. (See column 4 in table 4.10). The first moving average is 6.42, calculated thus:

$$6.42 = \frac{4.8 + 6.9 + 5.9 + 8.1}{4}$$

Table 4.6   Quarterly shipments

Quarter	Year 1973	1974	1975	1976	1977	1978	1979	1980	1981
1	4.8	6.6	7.0	10.3	15.1	13.6	19.5	23.1	23.6
2	6.9	9.5	10.8	18.4	18.8	19.4	28.4	31.0	34.6
3	5.9	7.9	9.3	15.8	15.4	17.7	26.0	26.0	31.3
4	8.1	10.6	14.7	19.9	19.7	26.1	34.4	34.4	36.7

Since it includes the first four actual observations, for time periods 1, 2, 3, 4, the moving average should really be centred between periods 2 and 3. Because the cyclical effect is calculated for each time period, each moving average must refer to one and only one time period. Arbritrarily, it is taken to refer to the later of the two periods, i.e. time period 3. Period 2 would have been equally approximate.

The second moving average incorporates the actual data from periods 2–5 and is centred on period 4. The last moving average is for period 35 and includes the last four items of actual data (periods 33–6).

Column 5 in table 4.10 shows the trend, calculated from the regression equation. For example, for 1976, quarter four (time period 16):

$$\text{trend} = 2.851 + 0.838 \times 16$$
$$= 16.26$$

The cyclical ratio (= moving average/trend = column 4/column 5) is shown in column 6. If this ratio exhibits any pattern, it should be revealed by drawing a graph relating the ratio to time, as in figure 4.4. There does appear to be a cycle of length 12 quarters, since troughs and peaks both recur at this interval. For each of the 12 periods within the cycle, this effect can be calculated by averaging over all such periods. The first period of the cycle is taken, arbitrarily, to be the first

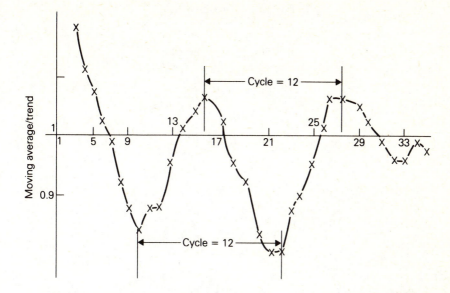

Figure 4.4 The cyclical ratio graphed against time.

period of the time series. The cyclical effect for, as an example period 5 of the cycle is calculated (using data from column 6 of table 4.10):

$$\begin{aligned}
\text{cyclical effect for period 5 of cycle} \\
= \text{average for periods 5, 17, 29} \\
= \frac{1.07 + 1.02 + 1.05}{3} \\
= 1.05
\end{aligned}$$

The effect for all 12 periods of a cycle is shown in table 4.7.

3 Calculate the seasonal effect. The seasonality is the ratio of actual to moving average, averaged for each quarter. Table 4.10 shows these ratios in column 7 calculated as column 3 divided by column 4. Average these ratios for the first quarter:

$$\begin{aligned}
\text{seasonality index for quarter 1} \\
= \frac{0.88 + 0.77 + 0.78 + 0.87 + 0.80 + 0.85 + 0.81 + 0.80}{8} \\
= 0.82
\end{aligned}$$

Table 4.7   Cyclical effect

Time period of cycle	Cyclical effect
1	0.96
2	1.01
3	1.10
4	1.08
5	1.05
6	1.00
7	0.97
8	0.92
9	0.89
10	0.89
11	0.91
12	0.88

Table 4.8 shows all four seasonal indices.

Table 4.8   Seasonal indices

Quarter	Basic seasonal index
1	0.82
2	1.14
3	0.93
4	1.21

Unfortunately, there is a difficulty with the basic seasonal indices shown in table 4.8. The overall effect is to change the level of data. Their average is different from 1.

$$\text{average seasonal effect} = \frac{0.82 + 1.14 + 0.93 + 1.21}{4}$$

$$= 1.025$$

The seasonal index is meant to re-arrange the pattern within a year, not to increase the trend. In the above case the trend would be increased by 2.5 per cent each year. The seasonal indices have to be adjusted so that their average is 1. This is done by dividing each index in table 4.8 by 1.025 to give the adjusted seasonal indices of table 4.9.

Table 4.9   Adjusted seasonal indices

Quarter	Adjusted seasonal index
1	0.80
2	1.11
3	0.91
4	1.18

The average seasonal effect is now neutral since:

$$\frac{0.80 + 1.11 + 0.91 + 1.18}{4} = 1.00$$

4 Make the forecasts. The original time series has now been decomposed into trend, cycle and seasonality. To make forecasts for 1983, the three elements are re-assembled. The forecasts are shown in table 4.11.

(a) The trend is $2.851 + 0.838 \times$ time. The four quarters of 1983 are the time periods numbered 41–4. The trend for the first quarter is therefore:

$$2.851 + 0.838 \times 41 = 37.21$$

(b) Each cycle lasts for 12 periods. Starting at the first quarter of 1973, the cycles are 1973–5, 1976–8, 1979–81. Consequently the four quarters of 1983 are time periods 5–8 of a cycle. The cyclical effects for these periods are taken from table 4.7.

(c) The seasonal effect for each quarter is taken from table 4.9. The forecast is the product of the three elements, e.g. for 1983, quarter 1:

$$\begin{aligned} forecast &= 37.21 \times 1.05 \times 0.80 \\ &= 31.26 \end{aligned}$$

Conclusion

This chapter has tried to show the types of data with which time series methods can deal. The techniques are just a few of the many that are available. Furthermore, the basic ideas can be extended to allow for a variety of circumstances. In particular, smoothing methods are capable of a wide range of applications. For example, they can

Table 4.10 The original time series decomposed into trend, cycle and seasonality

1973: 1	1	4.8	—	3.69	—	—
2	2	6.9	—	4.53	—	—
3	3	5.9	6.42	5.36	1.20	0.92
4	4	8.1	6.87	6.20	1.11	1.18
1974: 1	5	6.6	7.52	7.04	1.07	0.88
2	6	9.5	8.02	7.88	1.02	1.18
3	7	7.9	8.65	8.72	0.99	0.91
4	8	10.6	8.75	9.56	0.92	1.21
1975: 1	9	7.0	9.07	10.39	0.87	0.77
2	10	10.8	9.42	11.23	0.84	1.15
3	11	9.3	10.45	12.07	0.87	0.89
4	12	14.7	11.27	12.91	0.87	1.30
1976: 1	13	10.3	13.17	13.74	0.96	0.78
2	14	18.4	14.80	14.58	1.01	1.24
3	15	15.8	16.10	15.42	1.04	0.98
4	16	19.9	17.30	16.26	1.06	1.15
1977: 1	17	15.1	17.40	17.10	1.02	0.87
2	18	18.8	17.30	17.93	0.96	1.09
3	19	15.4	17.25	18.77	0.92	0.89
4	20	19.7	16.87	19.61	0.86	1.17
1978: 1	21	13.6	17.02	20.45	0.83	0.80
2	22	19.4	17.60	21.29	0.83	1.10
3	23	17.7	19.17	22.12	0.87	0.92
4	24	26.0	20.65	22.96	0.90	1.26
1979: 1	25	19.5	22.90	23.80	0.96	0.85
2	26	28.4	24.97	24.64	1.01	1.14
3	27	26.0	27.07	25.48	1.06	0.96
4	28	34.4	27.97	26.31	1.06	1.23
1980: 1	29	23.1	28.62	27.15	1.05	0.81
2	30	31.0	28.62	27.99	1.02	1.08
3	31	26.0	28.62	28.83	0.99	0.91
4	32	34.4	28.75	29.67	0.97	1.20
1981: 1	33	23.6	29.65	30.50	0.97	0.80
2	34	34.6	30.97	31.34	0.99	1.12
3	35	31.3	31.55	32.18	0.98	0.99
4	36	36.7	—	33.02	—	—

Table 4.11   Forecasts for 1983

Year/ Quarter	Trend	Cycle	Seasonality	Forecast
1983: q1	37.21	1.05	0.80	31.26
q2	38.05	1.00	1.11	42.24
q3	38.88	0.97	0.91	34.32
q4	39.72	0.92	1.18	43.12

cover the incorporation of judgement into the forecast (as in the Harrison–Stevens method). The Trigg–Leach tracking signal is a system for monitoring forecasting errors and checking whether they are random; adaptive response rate is a means of setting the smoothing constant automatically and altering it as time goes by and new data become available. Consult the Further Reading list (p. 193) for details of these and other methods.

In spite of the flexibility of time series methods and the fact that surveys have demonstrated how effective they can be, they are often undervalued. The reason is that, since a variable is predicted solely from its own historical record, the methods have no power to respond to changes in business or company conditions. They work on the assumption that circumstances will be as in the past.

Nevertheless, their track record is good, especially for short-term forecasting. In addition, they have one big advantage over other methods. Because they work solely from the historical record and do not necessarily require any element of judgement or forecasts of other causal variables, they can operate automatically. For example, a large warehouse, holding thousands of items of stock, has to predict future demands and stock levels. The number of items, which may be of low unit value, means that it is neither practicable nor economic to give each variable individual attention. Time series methods will provide good short-term forecasts by computer without needing managerial attention. Of course, some initial research would have to be carried out, for instance to find the best overall values of smoothing constants. But once this research was done, the forecasts could be made automatically. All that would be needed would be the updating of the historical record as new data became available. This should cause little difficulty if the stock system is computerized.

The conclusion is, therefore, that time series methods should not be underestimated. They have advantages of cost and, in the short term, of accuracy over other methods.

CHAPTER 5

The Role of Forecasts in Management Decisions

The Forecasting Trap

This chapter is about the forecasting trap and, in particular, how to avoid being caught by it.

The forecasting trap can occur whenever a forecast becomes an end in itself and not just a means to an end. What usually happens is that a management problem arises which cannot be solved until a good forecast of some trend or other is available. Management attention is consequently directed away from the problem and towards the forecast. So long as the purpose of the forecast is kept in mind, this is fine. Unfortunately, the purpose is sometimes forgotten and then the forecast often turns out to be both more accurate and more expensive than is really necessary.

The appealing approach, and the trap, is to concentrate first on the forecast and only to worry about the decision after the forecast is available. Unfortunately, out of its decision context, the only way to judge a forecast is in terms of its accuracy; the more accurate the better. However, in many practical cases, a more accurate forecast can make surprisingly little difference to the eventual decision.

There are, of course, exceptions to this, but the important point is that before indulging in an expensive forecasting exercise it is important to ask some fundamental questions:

Why is it needed?

What is it worth?

How would you cope without it?

Is it likely to change any decisions?

This last question is particularly important because even a very accurate forecast is worthless if, no matter what it says, the decision is left unchanged.

In order to find out how good a forecast you need it is necessary to look quite closely at the relationship between the decisions which have to be made and the forecasts which influence those decisions. As a start it is useful to consider two simple and obvious basic ideas which are the key to avoiding the forecasting trap.

Forecasts reduce but do not eliminate uncertainty. Anything that needs forecasting is by its nature uncertain. Even a good forecast will rarely eliminate that uncertainty completely; it will simply reduce it. Hence, with or without a forecast, the final decision must still allow for some degree of uncertainty.

Forecasts must be judged against prior knowledge not against ignorance. In most situations managers have a substantial fund of prior knowledge about the likelihood of different possible outcomes. Consequently, they can usually make a reasonably good decision even without a formal forecast. Thus a forecast must complement and enhance that prior knowledge. It is not good enough for it to be an improvement over complete ignorance.

As an illustration of these ideas, suppose that you have to make an urgent decision which requires a good forecast of next year's sales level. Unfortunately, no forecast is available, although you are fairly confident that the sales will be greater than £35m but less than £58m. Within this range some figures are obviously more likely than others. For example sales values in the middle of the range are probably more likely than values at either extreme. You might be able to go further and attach probabilities to different bands within the range as has been done in the central column of table 5.1. However, that is about the most you could do before facing the fact that you simply do not know exactly what the actual sales value will be. Consequently, you have no choice but to make an appropriate decision which takes account of the uncertainty.

That decision will naturally take advantage of the probability information given in table 5.1. Thus it need not make much allowance for the remote possibility that sales will be less than £39m or greater than £54m. Instead it would probably concentrate on the £43m–£50m band which is where the actual sales level is most likely to lie. On the other hand it is clear from table 5.1 that there is a very real chance (32

Table 5.1   Likelihood of different sales values actually occurring

Sales range (£m)	Estimated probability (%)	Revised probability (%)
Less than 35	Nil	Nil
35–38	2	3
39–42	14	7
43–46	34	28
47–50	34	45
51–54	14	16
55–58	2	Nil
More than 58	Nil	Nil

per cent) that sales will fall outside the most likely band, so it would be foolish to take no account of this possibility. For example, it might be appropriate to make some sort of contingency plan or to modify in some other way the optimal decision to allow for this uncertainty.

Even if a good quality sales forecast were available it is most unlikely that it would be able to say with complete certainty what sales next year were going to be. Instead it might be able to refine and tighten the original probabilities, hopefully bunching them more closely around the true value. For example, it might be that the forecaster could improve the original probability estimates given in the middle column of table 5.1 so as to produce the revised estimates shown in the right-hand column.

These revised probabilities should make the decision process easier but it is important to appreciate that they would not essentially change that process very much. In particular, the decision still has to take account of an uncertain future, albeit less uncertain than before. Thus the interesting question is whether the revised odds will result in a different and improved decision. If not, the forecast is worthless.

If the forecast would change the decision then it is meaningful to ask just how much that improvement is worth and hence it becomes possible to consider whether one forecast is worth more or less than another. In this way a criterion for distinguishing a good forecast from a bad one can be established.

Before looking in detail at the question of what a forecast is worth, a warning is in order. In practice, forecasting is not always seen as a revision of the odds in quite the way that has just been described.

One reason for this is that managers often do not give explicit thought to their pre-forecast view of the relevant probabilities. However, a more important reason is that managers are often unwilling to accept a forecast which refers to probabilities of different possible outcomes. Consequently, forecasters are often persuaded, usually against their better judgement, to provide the single most likely outcome as though it were the only possibility. This is obviously extremely dangerous because the best decision to deal with a certain future may be quite different from the equivalent decision to deal with an uncertain future.

In effect, the manager who accepts a single-point forecast is avoiding the reality of the situation and thereby avoiding managing. Consequently, it is preferable to take the view that a forecast is always about the probabilities associated with alternative possible outcomes. In particular, it is about the revision of poor estimates to produce better estimates.

What is a Forecast Worth?

The value of a forecast will inevitably change, depending on the circumstances. A forecast which can make a major improvement to a decision with a great deal of money at stake is worth more than one which has less impact on a decision involving less money. However, the precise relationship between the quality of the forecast and the associated decision is quite complicated and the theory can seem a great deal more difficult than it really is. A simple example will therefore be used to illustrate the main theoretical ideas and most of the important results.

Suppose the forecasts are required to help decide whether or not to buy a company. The price is £4m and the only significant assets are £2m cash and some rather dubious Central American bonds. The cash could be remitted immediately and invested to earn 15 per cent; the problem lies with the bonds. They have no market value but are due to mature in a year when they will be worth £9m. Unfortunately they are quite likely to default in which case they will be worth nothing.

There is no way of knowing whether or not the bonds will default but in the absence of an expert forecast a reasonable guess might be that the chance of default is as high as eight in ten. Fortunately expert help is at hand in the shape of two competing bond-rating services who, for a suitable fee, will provide an 'OK' or 'DUD' forecast for bonds of this kind.

In order to be sure of avoiding the forecasting trap it is a good idea to ask what decision should be made if no forecast was available. The various alternative outcomes have been listed in table 5.2. From this it is obvious that by next year you could be in one of three situations:

1 If you do not buy the company you will have the £4m, but by then it will have grown to £4.6m. This will occur whether the bond turns out to be good or bad.
2 If you buy the company and the bond does not default, you will then have £2.3m from the invested cash plus £9m from the bond; £11.3m in total.
3 If you buy the company but the bond defaults, you will only have left the £2.3m of invested cash.

Table 5.2   Decision pay-offs, in £m

Outcome	Estimated probability	Decision Buy	Don't buy	Best outcome
Bond good	0.2	11.3	4.6	11.3m
Bond bad	0.8	2.3	4.6	4.6m
Expected monetary value		4.1	4.6	5.94m

The optimal decision obviously depends critically on the probability of default, but without further information there is no alternative to using your own estimate of an 80 per cent chance of default. Thus the problem is reduced to asking whether you would rather have £4.6m with certainty or gamble £2.3m against £11.3m. Remember that you only have a 20 per cent chance of ending up with the £11.3m.

Since different people have different attitudes towards taking risks there is no simple answer to whether this risk is acceptable. However, one useful measure of a risky event is its 'expected monetary value', often called EMV. This is calculated by adding up each pay-off multiplied by its probability of occurrence. The result is a sort of weighted – average pay-off. In the present example the EMV of the investment works out to be $2.3 \times 0.8 + 11.3 \times 0.2 = 4.1$.

A good deal has been written about the relevance of EMV in situations like this one. It would seem that most people prefer a certain pay-off to a gamble with the same EMV. For example, most people would prefer a certain £100,000 to the chance of tossing a coin for nothing or £200,000. On the other hand, people vary a great deal in the amount they would accept to avoid the gamble. A cautious person might accept £50,000 or even less rather than toss the coin. A less risk-averse person might want to take a chance unless the certain alternative was at least £90,000.

It is theoretically possible to allow for personal differences in risk preference. This is done by converting the money pay-offs into 'utility units' and then working with expected utility rather than expected money. However, it is not easy to do this in practice and fortunately it is not usually necessary. This is because most businesses have many uncertain events outstanding at any time so the good outcomes tend to cancel out the bad. If this happens to any extent the EMV associated with each individual decision will become quite a good guide to the effect of that decision on the business as a whole.

The different risks will not entirely cancel out, so EMV is at best an approximation. Nevertheless, it may be a much better approximation than that which would result from making sophisticated adjustments for utility but ignoring the cancelling effect caused by diversification. In any event, throughout the rest of this chapter EMV will be used as a criterion for selecting between uncertain alternatives. It simplifies the exposition a good deal without significantly affecting the important points being made about the role of forecasting.

Returning to the example, it is clear that under the EMV assumption the investment company should not be purchased. Its EMV is only £4.1m compared with the certain alternative of £4.6m. However, it is interesting to ask whether this decision might be changed if a really good forecast of the bond's quality were available. The best possible forecast would obviously be completely accurate, so one might start by asking whether a perfect forecast would change the decision and if so what such an accurate forecast might be worth.

A completely accurate forecast saying the bond was 'OK' would, of course, guarantee a pay-off of £11.3m if the company was purchased. On the other hand, if the forecast said the bond was 'DUD' the company should not be purchased. Either way, the best decision could be made. Unfortunately, there is no way of knowing in advance which way the forecast will go.

The original estimate of default was 80 per cent so it follows that a 'DUD' signal can be expected with an 80 per cent probability. Similarly an 'OK' signal can be expected with a 20 per cent probability. Hence a perfect forecast would raise the EMV from 4.6 to $0.2 \times 11.3 + 0.8 \times 4.6 = 5.94$. So its value must be the increase from the original EMV to 5.94, that is $5.94 - 4.6 = 1.34$. No forecast can be better than perfect, so no forecast can possibly have a greater value than £1.34m.

A different way of looking at the value of a forecast is to ask whether it would ever cause you to change your original decision. The original decision was 'Don't buy' so a reliable forecast of 'DUD' would not cause you to change your mind. However, a reliable forecast of 'OK' would change your mind; you would now 'Buy' and increase your pay-off to £11.3m making a gain of 11.3 – 4.6 = 6.7.

An 'OK' forecast is not very likely, so the chance of making this gain is not very great. In fact it is only 20 per cent which means that the expected value of the gain is only $0.2 \times 6.7 = 1.34$. This figure is exactly the same as the one calculated previously but this time it has more intuitive appeal. Furthermore, it clearly illustrates one of the most important results of information theory. This states that the value of any forecasting system is the expected value of the gains from any changed decisions. The corollary naturally says that if there are no changed decisions then the forecasting system has no value.

In the real world, forecasts are not completely reliable. To investigate the value of a good but imperfect forecast in the present example, you might consider one of the available bond-rating services. The service is run by 'Old Harry' a very well informed financial consultant who specializes in Central American bonds. Old Harry is famous for never making a mistake with bad bonds. Unfortunately he has achieved this remarkable record by consistent pessimism which also affects his opinion of good bonds.

Given a good bond, Old Harry will only forecast it as 'OK' about 50 per cent of the time. Hence he gives a 'DUD' forecast much too often. This has two consequences. Firstly, it means that his forecasts are somewhat inaccurate, which raises the question of whether they are good enough to use. Secondly, if they are good enough to use, they must be worth less than a perfect forecast since he will supply the crucial 'OK' signal less often.

The first question is easy to answer. If Harry says 'OK' and consequently the company is purchased there is certain to be a gain because he only says 'OK' to good bonds. On the other hand, if he says 'DUD' and consequently the company is not purchased there is no gain but neither is there any loss because the company was not going to be purchased anyway. Thus there is some chance of gain and no chance of loss. Hence it is possible to say with confidence that Harry's forecasts are good enough to use.

It is slightly more difficult to discover the value of Harry's forecasts because it is not obvious how often he will actually admit to a bond being 'OK'. However, the figure is quite easy to work out because about 20 per cent of bonds are in fact good and to these he says 'OK' about 50 per cent of the time. Thus he will say 'OK' about 10 per cent of the time from which it follows that the value of his forecast is 10 per cent of the £6.7m gain: in other words £670,000. Thus, although in a sense he is very accurate, Harry will only rarely give a forecast which leads to any gain. Consequently the value of his forecast is quite a bit less than the value of a perfect forecast which was £1.34m.

The arithmetic to evaluate Harry's forecast required no more than common sense. As problems become more complicated this will no longer be true. A more systematic approach is required. Several alternatives exist but they all amount to variations on the same idea which is sometimes referred to as Bayes' theorem. Probably the easiest way to understand this is to use a tree diagram which can be illustrated by looking at another bond-rating service – Zetabond.

The Zetabond service is similar to Old Harry. It gives 'OK' and 'DUD' forecasts for Central American bonds although its methods are very different. In general the service is not as highly regarded as Old Harry but it is much less pessimistic. This is shown in the forecasters track record because given a good bond they will rate it 'OK' 75 per cent of the time and 'DUD' only 25 per cent of the time. The same optimism naturally spills over to bad bonds which they rate 'OK' 55 per cent of the time and 'DUD' only 45 per cent of the time.

The important difference from Old Harry is that Zetabond may give a wrong forecast whatever the true state of the bond; they may say that a good bond is 'DUD' or that a bad bond is 'OK'. Consequently, it is necessary to be rather more careful when calculating the various probabilities. This can be done by first writing down everything in a tree diagram as shown in figure 5.1. The probabilities shown in figure 5.1 provide a convenient summary of the historical track record but unfortunately they are not in a form that is of much practical use. This is because the forecast will be presented as 'OK' or 'DUD' but there will be no way of knowing whether the bond is really good or bad. It would be much better if figure 5.1 could be presented the other way round; that is, in a form where given an 'OK' or 'DUD' forecast, the probability of the bond actually being good or bad could be seen at a glance.

In order to achieve this turning round of the tree diagram it is first necessary to calculate the probability of each path through the tree. For example the first path follows the top line where the bond really is good and Zetabond says 'OK'. This has a probability of (20 per cent × 75 per cent = 15 per cent). These probabilities are usually called joint probabilities and in figure 5.1 are shown in parentheses at the extreme right of the diagram.

The overall probability of receiving an 'OK' or a 'DUD' signal can be

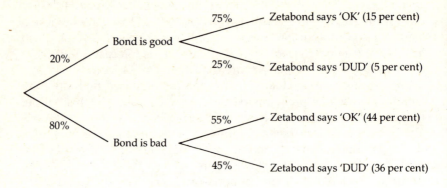

Figure 5.1   Historical record for Zetabond.

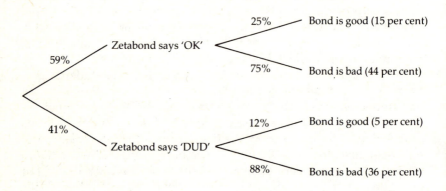

Figure 5.2   Revised probabilities for Zetabond.

calculated next by summing the appropriate joint probabilities. In the example these work out to be (15 per cent + 44 per cent = 59 per cent) for an 'OK' and (5 per cent + 36 per cent = 41 per cent) for a 'DUD'. The probability of receiving each signal can then be entered on the left-hand part of figure 5.2.

Once the probabilities of the various forecasts have been calculated it is a simple matter to finish off the diagram. The trick is to realize that the paths through the tree in figure 5.1 are essentially the same as the paths through the tree in figure 5.2. Hence the joint probabilities must be the same. Thus, for example, the event 'Bond bad/Zetabond says OK' must have exactly the same probability of occurrence whichever way round it is written. Consequently, the joint probabilities can be entered in figure 5.2 simply by copying them from figure 5.1. It will, however, be necessary to note that they appear in a different order in each diagram.

The final step of calculating the probability of each true state (good or bad) given each forecast ('OK' or 'DUD') is a matter of simple arithmetic. Once a specific signal such as 'OK' has been received, the bond can only be good or bad. Thus the probability of these two alternatives must sum to 1. They must also be in proportion to the joint probabilities. Hence to calculate the probability of the bond being good following an 'OK' signal it is only necessary to divide the joint probability (15 per cent) by the probability of receiving that signal (59 per cent). It works out to be 25 per cent and in the same way the probability of the bond being bad following an 'OK' signal works out to be 75 per cent.

The probabilities associated with a 'DUD' signal can be calculated in exactly the same way. Figure 5.2 shows these to be 12 per cent for a good bond and 88 per cent for a bad bond. However, since turning round the probability tree is important, but perhaps not immediately obvious, it might be a good idea to check these calculations for yourself.

When Zetabond's track record was first described it might not have been obvious that their forecasts had some serious shortcomings. Once the probabilities are turned round this becomes immediately apparent. They are giving 'OK' forecasts about three times too often. Hence when they do so they are wrong about 75 per cent of the time.

Despite being wrong rather often, there is some information content in Zetabond forecasts. This must be true because their forecasts have the effect of modifying the original probabilities. In the case of an 'OK' forecast, the original odds of 20:80 are modified to 25:75 and in the case of a 'DUD' forecast they are modified from 20:80 to 12:88. If their forecast had been completely useless, then whatever they said would have made no difference to the original probabilities. The logic behind this statement is probably obvious. If not, the best way to understand it is to assume that 'OK' and 'DUD' forecasts are determined by the forecaster tossing a coin and then completely rework the example.

If Zetabond's forecasts had no information content at all they would be completely worthless. This is because unchanged probabilities must imply unchanged decisions. However, their forecasts do have some information content; so the question is, what is their value. As usual this is easily discovered by asking in what circumstances the original decision would be changed and what the likelihood is of that change occurring.

Consider first a 'DUD' forecast. There is some chance that the bond is good but even so the EMV from buying the company following a 'DUD' forecast is only £3.38m ($0.12 \times 11.3 + 0.88 \times 2.3$). Since £3.8m is less than £4.6m there is no reason to change the original decision not to buy the company.

In the case of an 'OK' forecast, the probability of the bond being good is raised to 25 per cent which has the effect of raising the EMV to £3.55m ($0.25 \times 11.3 + 0.75 \times 2.3$). However, £3.55m is still less than £4.6m so even if Zetabond says the bond is 'OK' it is still better not to buy the company. Nothing that Zetabond says will cause the original decision to be changed so, despite having information content, their service is worthless in the context of the present decision.

This result leads to an important generalization. Information content, in the sense of modifying the prior probabilities, is a necessary condition for a forecasting system to have value. However, it is not a sufficient condition. In order to have value the information content must be powerful enough to cause a decision change to result from at least one of the possible forecasts that might be received.

The example of the investment company was perfectly adequate to illustrate the basic ideas of the role of forecasts in decision theory. However, it is not very typical of most forecasting problems so it is appropriate to consider a more conventional sales forecasting problem. This problem is a little more complicated than the previous one but it allows some new ideas to be explored.

The problem to be analysed concerns the decision to increase a product's price from its current level of £5 to a new price of £6. Sales volume is at present 18,000 units which generates revenue of £90,000 and profit of £32,000. If the price is held at £5 it is assumed that the same revenue and profit can be expected next year. This may be unrealistic but it simplifies the example and focuses attention on the more important issue of the sales forecast.

The range of different possible outcomes for the new price, including the relevant profit figures, are shown in table 5.3.

It is an easy matter, using the data given in table 5.3, to discover that the EMV of raising the price to £6 is only £30,500. The alternative of holding it at £5 offers £32,000 so the optimal action is not to raise the price. However, this decision might be altered if a more precise sales forecast was available. Bert, the sales manager, is prepared to carry out a market survey so we next need to consider whether this would be a good idea.

Table 5.3 Probabilities and profits of alternative sales levels

Possible sales levels if price = £6 (000 units)	Estimate of probability (%)	Profit if price = £6 (£000)	Profit if price = £5 (£000)
16	10	40	32
15	30	35	32
14	30	30	32
13	20	25	32
12	10	20	32
	100		

This is not an appropriate place to discuss the analysis and appraisal of market surveys. Instead, simply assume that an analysis of Bert's track record has enabled the probabilities in table 5.4 to be calculated. They show the relationship between the possible forecasts and the actual outcomes. Clearly the forecasts have some information content. In all cases they alter the original probabilities and tighten them up around the correct values. Nevertheless, as explained above, information content is not enough. The crucial question is whether any of the forecasts would lead to a changed decision.

Table 5.4 Probabilities revised in the light of the sales manager's forecasts

Sales levels (000 units)	Bert forecasts (% probability)					Original estimate
	16	15	14	13	12	
16	16	17	8	6	0	10
15	46	39	24	18	30	30
14	23	26	32	38	30	30
13	15	9	26	25	20	20
12	0	9	10	13	20	10
Total	100	100	100	100	100	100

When the EMVs are calculated, it turns out that the forecasts are good enough to use. The only sales levels that would lead to a profit increase are 16,000 and 15,000. If Bert forecasts either of these then the EMV from raising the price exceeds £32,000. On the other hand, if Bert forecasts 12,000, 13,000 or 14,000, which are the actual outcomes that would make you worse off, then the EMVs work out to be less than £32,000. Unfortunately, an outcome of 15,000 or 16,000 is not very likely and Bert's forecasts, although useful, are far from perfect. Indeed it is worth confirming, as an exercise, that the value of Bert's survey is only £230.

Forecasting as a Decision

Sometimes, for administrative or technical reasons, the forecasting and decision-making processes are quite distinct. The forecaster finds himself trying to provide relevant forecasts but having very little idea of the decision context within which they were going to be used.

The most sensible approach in this circumstance is to assume that no-one is likely to. lose money by believing a completely accurate forecast. However, it is reasonable to assume that money could be lost by using an inaccurate forecast. Probably, the more inaccurate the forecast, the greater the amount that could be lost. Thus what the forecaster tries to do is design a forecasting system which minimizes the expected amount of money lost.

There are a number of different ways of relating the size of the error to the amount of money assumed to be lost and this relationship is sometimes known as the *loss function*. The most common loss function, and the one that underlies most statistics theory, assumes that the loss is proportional to the square of the error. This means that large errors are penalized very much more heavily than small ones; doubling the error implies quadrupling the loss. Nevertheless, there are other possibilities. In different circumstances it may be preferable to assume the loss is proportional to the absolute size of the error, or perhaps the percentage error. These alternatives are generally less common than the squared error but they may be preferable if they provide a better match with the real decision for which the forecast is being used.

As an illustration of forecasting seen as a decision process let us consider a variation of the previous sales forecasting example. In contrast to the original problem, suppose that nothing is known about the pay-offs to be expected in different circumstances. Instead, the best forecast has to be selected using a loss function. The absolute error and squared error alternatives are set out in tables 5.5. Apart from using the loss function instead of the actual pay-offs, the remaining facts are unchanged.

The difficult question is how best to integrate your own opinion with Bert's forecast. For example, if he says 15,000 should you pass

Table 5.5   Absolute error and squared error loss functions
Loss proportional to absolute error:

Actual sales (000 units)	Forecast 16	15	14	13	12
16	0	1	2	3	4
15	1	0	1	2	3
14	2	1	0	1	2
13	3	2	1	0	1
12	4	3	2	1	0

Loss Proportional to squared error:

Actual sales (000 units)	Forecast 16	15	14	13	12
16	0	1	4	9	16
15	1	0	1	4	9
14	4	1	0	1	4
13	9	4	1	0	1
12	16	9	4	1	0

that on as your forecast or should you modify it in some way? In decision terms your options are to pass on one of five opinions: 16,000, 15,000, 14,000, 13,000 or 12,000.

Without Bert's help you would choose 14,000. Given the original probability estimates this minimizes the expected loss, assuming either loss function. However, once Bert has forecast 15,000 the original probabilities are no longer the best available. Instead the revised probabilities shown in table 5.4 can be used. In this case, using the absolute error loss function, it turns out that the best forecast is 15,000. In other words, passing on Bert's forecast of 15,000 minimizes the expected loss.

An interesting situation arises if the calculations are repeated for the squared error loss function, because the previous optimal forecast of 15,000 now becomes 14,000. This surprising result is a consequence of the different ways in which the two loss functions evaluate large errors. If actual sales are 12,000 then a forecast of 15,000 leads to a much larger error than would have resulted from a forecast of 14,000. The absolute error loss function does not penalize this too severely and it only leads to a loss of 3. However, the squared error loss function regards it as a disaster and assigns a loss of 9. Consequently, in one case the benefits of greater accuracy in the likely range outweigh the increased risk of a large error. In the other case they do not.

The Role of Prior Probabilities

Throughout this chapter a very significant role has been taken by the original probability estimates or 'prior probabilities' as they are usually called. It is an unfortunate fact that if they had been different, even by quite small amounts, the results could easily have been changed. Yet frequently these important figures are difficult to discover and managers are most reluctant to provide even rough figures. Thus it is appropriate to conclude this chapter with a closer look at prior probabilities.

Consider again the example of Old Harry and Zetabond at the beginning of the chapter and assume now that you already have a Zetabond forecast of 'OK' before you go to see Old Harry. Bear in mind that the Zetabond forecast is worthless because it does not make you change your decision. Nevertheless it does slightly change your view of the relative probabilities (from 20:80 to 25:75). Hence, when analysing the value of Old Harry's forecast you would do so with revised prior probabilities of 25:75. This naturally changes all the arithmetic a little but it still suggests that you should follow Harry's advice; if he says the bond is 'OK' you should buy, but if he says it is 'DUD' you should not. The interesting difference is that in the new situation the value of Harry's forecast is increased from its previous value of £670,000 to £850,000. This means that by first acquiring a worthless forecast you can apparently add £180,000 to the value of Harry's forecast!

Most people intuitively find this result unreasonable. But whether or not it is correct depends on Harry's and Zetabond's forecasts being independent of each other. Suppose, in the extreme case, that Harry actually receives Zetabond's forecasts. Then, by pooling the two forecasts, you are effectively double counting information that he has already taken into account.

Even without this extreme assumption it is quite likely that Harry and Zetabond use more or less the same information sources. If so, there will be a very high chance that they will frequently come to similar conclusions. The information is no longer independent and if you combine it you are still double counting, albeit in a less obvious way. The only circumstance under which it would be correct to combine the forecasts and genuinely achieve the value increase would be if the two forecasts were statistically completely independent. This amounts to saying that the two forecasts must be uncorrelated.

An uncomfortable extension of the same idea is to ask whether the likely dependence between Harry and Zetabond does not equally apply to your own prior probability estimate. The answer must be that it depends on the source of your prior probabilities. If the probabilities were subjective and based on broadly the same information sources then you will be double counting. On the other hand, if your prior probabilities were objectively based on the historical default record of Central American bonds then your estimate might well be independent of the forecasts.

Conclusion

The main message of this chapter has been that forecasts are not very different from most other resources which managers have to acquire. In particular, it is perfectly meaningful to judge forecasts in terms of value for money. Their value, of course, will vary from situation to situation but, as with other resources, this value can be calculated by comparing the profits available with and without the forecast. Unfortunately this calculation involves questions about probability and uncertainty which most people find conceptually difficult. Nevertheless, because the value of a forecast does vary with the circumstances, it is really quite important to be aware of the issues involved.

One difference between managing forecasts and other business resources is that the problem is rarely a simple matter of choosing between forecast A and forecast B. Instead, it is much more often concerned with making the best use of forecast B given that forecast A is already available. This requires a fair amount of technical knowledge as well as good judgement. However, the general principle is that the contribution each source of information should be allowed to make depends on two factors: firstly, the confidence which can be placed in its accuracy, and secondly, the extent to which it contains independent rather than repeated information.

CHAPTER 6

Recognizing Good and Bad Forecasts

It is not easy to tell a good forecast from a bad one. Indeed, it can seem to be an impossible task when the reasoning behind each forecast is convincing and each is supported by expert opinion. Nevertheless, we shall suggest in this chapter that it is possible to distinguish between forecasts so long as a systematic approach is used. Furthermore, we shall show that the appraisal does not require a great deal of technical knowledge and that broadly the same approach applies in most forecasting situations.

The basic idea is that there are three important attributes against which any forecasting system can be judged. A good forecast will score well on all of them, whereas a poor forecast will score badly.

1 The forecast should have a good historical track record.
2 Its statistical and theoretical foundations should be sound; otherwise there is a real risk of the model suddenly failing to forecast accurately despite a good track record.
3 The forecasting system must be appropriate for the situation in which it is being used.

In order to make the discussion of these attributes as realistic as possible we shall examine a choice between alternative sales forecasts for a real company. The company is Gomme Holdings plc who manufacture good quality domestic furniture (G Plan) mostly for the UK market.

In November 1982 Gomme published its latest results which showed sales for the first half of 1982 to have been £10.7m. Using only information that would have been publicly available at that date, nine alternative forecasts were made of the half-yearly sales which might be expected during the following three periods. These forecasts are shown in table 6.1. They dramatically illustrate the large variations

Table 6.1   Alternative sales forecasts for
Gomme Holdings plc, in £m

Forecast	1982: 2	1983: 1	1983: 2
A	16.3	16.7	17.2
B	16.6	17.3	17.8
C	18.5	19.1	19.4
D	21.0	22.0	22.6
E	14.6	11.3	15.2
F	14.0	11.5	14.6
G	11.0	11.0	11.0
H	10.9	10.4	9.8
I	10.3	9.4	8.5

which can sometimes arise when very different approaches are applied to the same forecasting problem.[1]

The task is to try to choose the best forecast from amongst the nine. Since the actual outcome of these sales values is now known it will be possible to gain some further information by looking back at them with the wisdom of hindsight.

Does the Forecasting Model Have a Good Track Record?

The first task in assessing the track record of a forecasting system is to collect as many observations as possible of past forecast values, together with their corresponding actual outcomes. If the forecasting system has been in use for some time it should be possible to find the forecasts that were made at different dates in the past. Comparing these with the actual outcomes will obviously provide a genuine and very satisfactory way of assessing the track record. Unfortunately it is not always possible.

When actual forecasts do not exist, for example where a new forecasting system is being examined, it is necessary to try to calculate what the model would have forecast. This is not entirely satisfactory because a new model is almost certain to have been estimated using the data of the recent past. Consequently, testing it using that same data is likely to give over-optimistic results.

A further problem arising with calculated rather than actual forecasts is the choice of input values. If a real forecast requires an input value, such as the future inflation rate, it will use the best available

Table 6.2   Comparison of forecast and actual sales, in £m

	Actual	Forecast A	Forecast E
1971: 2	5.5	5.7	5.2
1972: 1	4.6	6.2	4.0
1972: 2	6.1	6.6	5.6
1973: 1	6.4	7.1	6.4
1973: 2	7.5	7.6	7.7
1974: 1	7.4	8.1	6.2
1974: 2	8.1	8.6	8.4
1975: 1	8.4	9.0	8.4
1975: 2	11.3	9.5	8.8
1976: 1	10.9	10.0	10.5
1976: 2	12.3	10.5	14.1
1977: 1	11.3	11.0	12.4
1977: 2	12.6	11.4	13.9
1978: 1	12.3	11.9	13.1
1978: 2	15.1	12.4	14.0
1979: 1	15.1	12.9	13.2
1979: 2	17.9	13.4	18.1
1980: 1	15.9	13.8	16.4
1980: 2	12.4	14.3	16.1
1981: 1	12.0	14.8	15.4
1981: 2	13.7	15.3	12.9
1982: 1	10.7	15.8	13.0

forecast. However, with hindsight it is possible and usually much easier to use the actual value. This makes sense because it allows the forecaster to identify errors in the model separately from errors in the input forecasts. Nevertheless, the use of accurate inputs in place of forecast inputs is likely to make the track record look better than it would have been in real life.

In the example, it is assumed that actual forecasts are not available so forecasts of the past have to be calculated by applying the forecasting rules to the appropriate past data. Table 6.2 shows two such forecasts: one for forecast A and one for forecast E. The precise calculation of these figures would obviously require detailed knowledge of how each forecasting system works. However, to explain that at the moment might prejudice later discussion so it is better to assume that the track record figures shown in table 6.2 were provided by the forecasters themselves. They would almost certainly have had to calculate them in the forecasting process, so the assumption is reasonable.

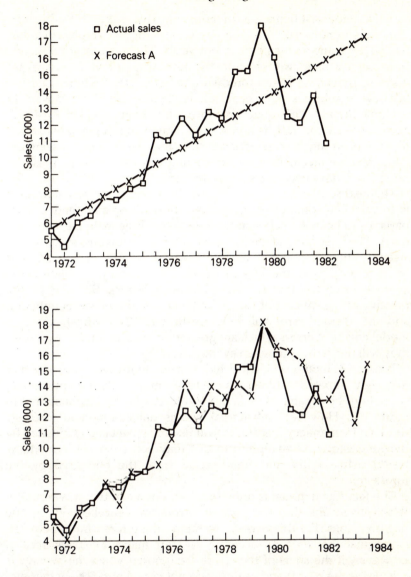

Figure 6.1 Graphing actual against forecast figures for Gomme Holdings plc: forecast A (top) and forecast E (bottom).

Once the past period forecasts have been assembled, the next step is to compare them with the actual values; these are also shown in table 6.2. A simple way of making the comparison is to graph the actual and forecast figures, as in figure 6.1. This makes it clear, just by visual inspection, that A uses a simple straight-line graph which has looked very unconvincing in recent years. The most recent forecasts have been a long way out and the turning point in 1979 was not noticed. Indeed, A is still forecasting a rising trend whereas for the last few years sales have been falling. If this falling trend were to continue through 1983, quite large forecasting errors could be expected. Forecast E, by contrast, is much more convincing. It generally seems to have been much more accurate than forecast A. Also, it seems to contain some mechanism for forecasting turning points as these, in most cases, have been correctly identified.

The next step, after visually comparing forecast and actual figures, is to calculate some error measures. These allow quantitative comparisons to be made between the forecasts. Three main measures are used. The first aims to discover whether a forecasting system consistently shoots too high or too low. Such a forecast is usually referred to as 'biased' and the bias is easily measured by calculating the average error (or the average percentage error). So long as the positive errors cancel out the negative errors, the model is unbiased and the average error will be close to zero. By contrast, a biased model will have errors which are greater on one side than the other so they will not cancel out when averaged.

Bias can sometimes be corrected. Consequently, a model which at first sight appears to forecast very badly may, with the appropriate correction, be capable of making good forecasts. This is illustrated in figure 6.2. However, substantial bias is not common in forecasts received by managers because it will usually have been eliminated by the forecasters. An exception to this may occur when the model is tested using a different time period from the one used by the forecaster.

The fact that a model is unbiased does not mean that it is accurate. It simply means that the positive errors are cancelled out by the negative ones. For this reason, averaging the errors cannot help you distinguish between an accurate and an inaccurate track record. However, if the signs of the errors are ignored when the average is calculated the pluses and minuses do not cancel out. A new measure results which measures how wrong the forecast was on average, irrespective of whether it overshot or undershot. This measure is called the mean absolute deviation or, more commonly, the MAD.

An alternative to the MAD is the mean squared error (MSE) which squares the error before averaging. Since the square of a positive or a negative number is positive, this also has the effect of not allowing

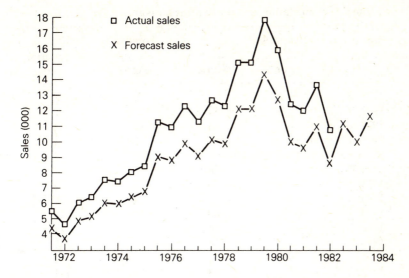

Figure 6.2   A biased forecast which could be accurate if appropriately corrected.

positive and negative errors to cancel each other out. The MSE has less intuitive appeal than the MAD. Nevertheless, for theoretical reasons statisticians often prefer it, although this is no reason to assume that MSE is always the better measure.

The crucial difference between MSE and MAD is in the treatment of large errors. When two errors are squared their relative difference increases, so using the MSE makes large errors appear to be more serious than they would appear using MAD. Hence the correct choice must depend on the circumstances. This was discussed more fully in chapter 5 where it was explained that the essential issue is the trade-off between error size and consequent financial loss.

Choosing a forecasting system by concentrating on the MSE implicitly assumes that doubling the forecast error will quadruple the consequent loss. By contrast, concentrating on the MAD implicitly assumes that the consequent loss is proportional to the size of the error, so that doubling the error merely doubles the loss. In addition both make an assumption, which may be unrealistic, that under-shooting and overshooting by the same amount leads to the same loss.

In practice, these measures are sometimes calculated using the actual error and sometimes using the percentage error. Statisticians

Table 6.3   Calculation of forecast error measures

	Forecast A		Forecast E	
	% error	Squared % error	% error	Squared % error
1971: 2	3	12	−6	38
1972: 1	34	1164	−12	147
1972: 2	9	84	−7	55
1973: 1	+11	110	−1	1
1973: 2	1	2	2	4
1974: 1	9	76	−16	264
1974: 2	6	40	5	22
1975: 1	7	55	0	0
1975: 2	−15	240	−22	476
1976: 1	−9	74	−4	17
1976: 2	−15	214	−15	215
1977: 1	−3	7	10	101
1977: 2	−9	88	10	101
1978: 1	−3	7	7	50
1978: 2	−18	321	−7	54
1979: 1	−15	230	−13	169
1979: 2	−25	642	1	1
1980: 1	−13	168	3	10
1980: 2	16	248	30	913
1981: 1	24	572	29	834
1981: 2	12	143	−6	34
1982: 1	47	2220	21	446

Forecast A		Forecast E	
Bias	= 2.5%	Bias	= 1.7%
MAD	= 13.8%	MAD	= 10.4%
MSE	= 305.3	MSE	= 179.6
$\sqrt{\text{MSE}}$	= 17.5%	$\sqrt{\text{MSE}}$	= 13.4%

N.B.   Figures in this table are accurately calculated from the original data. Using the rounded data shown in table 6.2 will lead to significant differences in some cases.

tend to prefer the former but the latter is often more intuitive and easier to use. This is particularly true when the data series is growing under the influence of inflation, as it is in this example.

The actual calculation of these measures is quite straightforward and the relevant figures are shown in table 6.3. First the percentage errors have to be calculated from the figures given in table 6.2. Then the percentage errors are averaged to calculate the bias. Next the

MAD is calculated, again by averaging, but this time ignoring the sign. Finally the percentage errors are squared and the squares are averaged to calculate the MSE. The square root of MSE is usually more meaningful than the MSE itself because its units are the same as the MAD and the bias so this figure is also shown in table 6.3.

The measures calculated in table 6.3 show that both forecasts have slight positive bias, although E is less biased than A. Also, as expected from the visual inspection, both MAD and $\sqrt{MSE}$ are smaller for E than for A. On average the E forecasts have been less wrong than the A forecasts. Nevertheless, it would be wrong to expect even E's forecasts to be completely accurate.

As a rough rule of thumb one can expect an error as large as the $\sqrt{MSE}$ to happen about one time in three and an error as bad as twice $\sqrt{MSE}$ to occur about one time in 20. Since these figures work out to be plus or minus 13.4 per cent and plus or minus 26.8 per cent for forecast E, there is obviously some substantial chance of making a serious error. It would also be wrong to interpret the figures as saying that E always forecasts better than A. It does on average, but not on every single occasion as inspection of table 6.2 will show.

Equivalent figures for the other forecasts have been calculated and the results are summarized in table 6.4. From these it is clear that E scores quite well and F, G and H are also fairly good. By contrast, forecasts A, B, C and D appear to have rather poor track records and can probably be rejected without too much further consideration.

Will the Model's Good Track Record Continue in the Future?

The fact that a forecasting system has worked well in the past does not guarantee that it will work well in the future. A good track record is an encouraging sign but it is still necessary to ask whether the system might forecast less well in the future than it has in the past. Naturally this is not easy, but there are warning signs. As a general rule, one should never trust a model unless it has both a sound statistical foundation and a sound theoretical foundation. Let us consider the statistical aspect first.

When a forecasting model is estimated certain assumptions have to be made about the nature of the underlying statistical process. In particular, the statistician assumes that the actual observations were generated by a combination of a systematic process and a random element. The systematic aspects should be completely captured by the model so the observed errors should be truly random. However,

Table 6.4   Comparison of percentage error measures for different forecasts

Forecast	Bias	MAD	MSE	$\sqrt{MSE}$
A	2.5	13.8	305.3	17.5
B	2.2	17.1	459.2	21.4
C	2.0	16.7	529.3	23.0
D	3.7	19.1	798.5	28.3
E	1.7	10.4	179.7	13.4
F	2.2	10.8	271.1	16.4
G	−3.8	12.9	247.5	15.7
H	0.3	12.0	243.1	15.6
I	−1.3	12.9	305.0	17.5

if the observed errors are not random it means that the underlying process cannot have been correctly specified. There are two implications arising from this.

One is that a better model must exist and the other is that the methods used to estimate the model were probably inappropriate. Both these problems may be serious, because an alarming characteristic of mis-specified models is that they appear to work quite well in their estimation period but suddenly collapse when used 'for real'.

Establishing whether or not the historical errors are random is a fairly technical question and managers should be able to leave it to the professionals. Nevertheless, the basic ideas are straightforward and can be easily understood. Firstly, there should be no tendency for the errors to get larger in recent periods, as for example, they seem to do for forecast A in table 6.3. Secondly, there should be no time series pattern in the errors. Subtle patterns may be hard to detect by eye and you may need powerful computer programs to find them. Nevertheless, there is a rough but quick test of randomness which requires no more than counting the number of times the errors change sign from plus to minus. This is equivalent to the runs test described in chapter 3: the number of sign changes is one fewer than the number of runs.

In a random series, adjacent errors should be independent, so there should be roughly half as many sign changes as there are observations. Of course you would not expect the figure to be exactly half. Nevertheless it can be shown[2] that in a random series the number of sign changes should be in the range $(0.5N \pm \sqrt{N})$, where N is one less than the number of observations.

By this standard forecast A looks most unconvincing. There are 22 observed errors, so the acceptable number of sign changes would be in the range 6 to 15. Yet there are only two changes of sign: one in 1972: 2 and the other in 1980: 2. Consequently, one must conclude that A is not well specified and there is some pattern in the errors which a better model could have detected. Forecast E, on the other hand, has nine changes of sign, which is perfectly acceptable.

Even if the errors look convincing, this is by no means the end of the story. It is surprisingly easy for a model to fit the data of the recent past extremely well and yet still not work in the future. This is because the forecaster has a huge number of options when building the forecasting model and he can easily be excessively influenced by the actual data of the recent past. In other words, he can easily build a model which fits the actual idiosyncrasies of recent data rather than identifying the underlying process.

Modern computer methods are so powerful that they can keep trying alternative models until they find one that fits the data well. For example, by using sufficiently complicated models it is possible to produce a well-fitting model of virtually any time series. This does not mean that the same complicated model would necessarily continue to work well in the future. Indeed, it is often the case that a simpler model will forecast the future as well as a more complicated one. But the simpler model will rarely fit the past as well because it will not be able to adapt so easily to the specific idiosyncrasies.

There is another side to this problem. While trying to stop the model from being excessively influenced by particular features of the recent past it is easy to introduce other biases. The worst case is when a forecaster or a manager rejects all evidence as eccentric unless it supports his own opinions. However, essentially the same issue arises in a less extreme form whenever a forecaster has to deal with an outlying observation. If it really is atypical, then excluding the outlier will improve the fit of the model and get closer to the underlying structure. On the other hand, if the observation is not eccentric, excluding it may reject vital evidence that the model is mis-specified. For example, it would be very tempting, but probably quite wrong, to reject the latest sales figure in forecast A as eccentric.

The only satisfactory way of checking that a forecasting system is more than just a description of the past is to carry out an independent test with data that were not used in its estimation. This means that some of the data must be held on one side and not allowed to influence the forecaster in any way. The best way to do this is a matter of considerable debate among statisticians. Holding out data for the latest few periods provides a convincing test but it also stops

Table 6.5   Comparison of hold-out period forecast errors

	1982: 2	1983: 1	1983: 2
Actual sales	14.0	12.4	14.5
Forecast – % errors			
A	16.5	35.1	18.6
B	19.1	39.5	22.5
C	32.7	54.3	33.4
D	50.8	77.5	55.6
E	4.5	−8.6	5.0
F	0.3	−7.2	0.6
G	−21.2	−11.2	−24.2
H	−21.6	−16.3	−32.6
I	−25.9	−23.9	−41.4

the most relevant data from being used in the forecast. Simple alternatives are to hold out a few early years or a few random years; but much more sophisticated hold-out techniques also exist.

In the example, the three latest observations were held on one side to provide an independent test of the forecasting methods. They are shown in table 6.5 along with the percentage errors that each forecast made. As one would expect from their track records, A performs rather worse than E.

A more interesting comparison is between F and H. The historical performance of both these forecasts was quite similar but, when given independent data, F managed to forecast with remarkable accuracy. H performed much worse than would have been expected from its track record. In due course we shall see how this surprising result might have been anticipated. For now all we can say is that H appears to be mis-specified. In the same way, C and D appear to be forecasting much worse in the hold-out period than would be indicated by their track records.

Apart from being influenced too much by the idiosyncrasies of the sample period there is a different problem which can produce very similar consequences. This occurs when there is a structural change during the estimation period so that the forecaster identifies either an out-of-date situation or else a meaningless hybrid of the old and the new. In the Gomme example this appears to be a distinct possibility. Firstly, it would explain why so many of the forecasts perform badly in the hold-out period. But also, from the sales graph in figure 6.1 the pattern does look as though it might be different before and after about 1978. The trend in the later period is falling rather than rising. In fact, a trend line using only the data beyond 1978 forecasts much better than a trend line for the whole period.

The possibility of structural change presents the forecaster with a difficult choice. He must balance the benefits of long data runs against the risk that earlier observations were generated in a different environment from the present. He faces a similar risk with inconsistent data. The longer the time period, the greater is the chance that earlier and later data will be inconsistent. In either case the manager who has a detailed knowledge of the business environment and of the data generation process will be in a strong position to judge whether the forecaster has coped adequately with these problems.

Before leaving the question of the statistical foundations of a forecast, it is worth giving some thought to the precise statistical techniques that have been used. In most situations some techniques would be preferable to others, but usually several alternatives will make sense. Thus it is worth investigating exactly which methods were used and perhaps also which methods were considered but rejected.

The example provided in chapter 9 provides a detailed illustration of how to confirm that the assumptions and circumstances under which the chosen method works best do indeed apply to the problem in hand. Of course, the experts can usually be trusted to have made the appropriate choice. Nevertheless, a forecaster will sometimes favour a method that he knows well to the exclusion of preferable alternatives. Also, some techniques are rather more expensive to implement than others so it may be sensible for the manager to show an interest in the choice even when he has little technical knowledge of the differences between them.

Does the Forecasting Model Make Sense?

Once you are satisfied that a forecasting system has a sound statistical foundation, it is time to consider its theoretical foundations. This involves confirming that the model represents a plausible theory of the underlying process. It also requires some thought to be given to whether circumstances might exist that would cause the model to fail and if so to the likelihood of such circumstances. Finally, the model's inputs should be checked to ensure that they will be available when needed and, if they require forecasting, that this can be done satisfactorily.

There are two aspects determining whether a model is theoretically plausible. Firstly, the input assumptions that it uses must be plausible and secondly, the model structure itself must be a good representation of the underlying process. Both are important because the same model used with different assumptions may give very different forecasts and similarly different models used with the same assumptions may give very different forecasts.

In most cases there will be several alternative values that might have been used for the input assumptions. Hence it is important to check which were actually used. For example, forecast F is based on the relationship that exists between the percentage change in real sales and the percentage change in real GDP. To turn this into a sales forecast requires a forecast of the percentage increase in GDP as well as a forecast of the inflation rate. If either of these forecasts is poor it would be unrealistic to expect a good sales forecast to result.

A particular problem arises when using macroeconomic forecasts because, by convention, they are typically based on unchanged government policy. Frequently this assumption is not plausible but to discover the impact of alternative policies it will be necessary to read the text carefully. Some forecasts, such as the LBS *Economic Outlook*, do make forecasts based on the most likely government policies. Even so, major events such as the outcome of an election may have a significant impact. Consequently, it is always important to be aware of any critical input assumptions that have been used. If possible, try to find out whether using different assumptions would have made much difference.

When investigating the plausibility of a model's structure, the first question to ask is whether the underlying process is better characterized by a time series model or a causal regression model. This really depends on whether or not a few key external influences are likely to be of predominant importance. For example, would the series be significantly affected by a change in aggregate consumers' expenditure, or the birth rate, or oil prices, or new housing? If this seems likely it is probably best to take those influences explicitly into account by means of a causal regression model.

In addition to selecting the external variables for a regression model it is also necessary to specify the precise relationship. For example, it might be best to use the actual values of the variables or it might be better to use their period-to-period changes. Alternatively, it might be better to use percentage changes as is the case for forecast F. A similar issue is how to handle variables which are subject to inflation; should actual data or inflation-adjusted data be used?

These matters may appear to be fairly minor but a comparison of forecasts B, D and E shows that they can be quite significant. Table 6.6 outlines the methodology behind the different forecasts and shows that forecast B started by calculating a regression between actual sales and actual GDP. Then it plugged a forecast for GDP into the regression to provide the sales forecast. The regression fit was apparently quite good (R squared $= 0.63$) and the GDP forecasts were good so it may seem a little surprising that both the track record and the forecast are rather poor.

Table 6.6   Summary of forecast methods used in the example

Forecast	Forecast method
A	Historical trend of actual sales used to forecast actual sales.
B	Regression calculated relating actual sales to actual gross domestic product. Forecast of actual GDP used in the regression to forecast actual sales.
C	Historical trend of inflation-adjusted (real) sales used to forecast real sales. Forecast of inflation used to convert real sales back to actual sales.
D	Regression calculated relating real sales to real GDP. Forecast of real GDP used in the regression to forecast real sales. Forecast of inflation used to convert real sales to actual sales.
E	Regression calculated relating year-on-year percentage growth in real sales to year-on-year percentage growth in real GDP. Forecast of percentage growth in real GDP used in regression to forecast percentage growth in real sales. Forecast of inflation used to convert percentage growth in real sales to percentage growth in actual sales. Percentage growth in actual sales used with prior year actual sales to calculate forecast actual sales.
F	As E except that the real consumers' expenditure used in place of real GDP.
G	Single exponential smoothing applied to the actual sales series and used to forecast actual sales.
H	As G but using double exponential smoothing.
I	As G but using Holt's method of smoothing.

The problem with forecast B is that its model is theoretically unsound. Both actual sales, and actual GDP are heavily influenced by inflation. Hence inflation enters both sides of the regression equation and causes the R squared to be spuriously high. The true relationship between inflation-adjusted (real) sales and real GDP is not nearly as good. In fact this was calculated for forecast D and the revised R squared is zero. In other words, apart from inflation there is no underlying relationship at all.

Forecast E also uses the inflation-adjusted figures and so is not subject to the problem of spuriously good results. However, in contrast to D it uses the year-on-year percentage changes of the variables, rather than their levels. This often works well and here it improves the R squared from zero to 0.49, which indicates a moderate but genuine relationship. Nevertheless, before this regression can be regarded as a plausible model it is necessary to establish whether its coefficients make sense. If they do not, there is strong evidence of mis-specification.

The precise regression equation is:

$$\text{Percentage growth in real sales} = -6.9 + 3.9 \times \text{percentage growth in real GDP}$$

This indicates that each additional 1 per cent increase in real GDP should lead to an additional 3.9 per cent increase in real sales. Since the demand for furniture is notoriously sensitive to upswings and downswings in the economy, this high figure is quite plausible. However, the negative constant is more surprising. It indicates that even if real GDP were unchanged Gomme's real sales would fall by around 6.9 per cent. In other words, it suggests that the company may be losing its market share. Unfortunately, with increased competition from overseas suppliers this is also quite plausible. Hence both regression coefficients can be regarded as plausible.

If the other regression-based forecasts (A to F) are reviewed in the same way it turns out that only E and F are acceptable. A and B both use figures not adjusted for inflation which gives them high but spurious R squared values. Equivalent regressions corrected for inflation (C and D) show that the whole of the apparent relationship in A and B is caused by inflation. What is left fits much too badly to be considered as a causal model. The last two models (E and F) are very similar to each other except that one is based on GDP whereas the other is based on consumer expenditure. Both fit reasonably well and both have plausible coefficients. The regression model and track record of E is slightly better. On the other hand F's use of consumer expenditure is more plausible and its performance in the hold-out period was very good. Hence it is not clear which should be preferred.

Regression or Time Series?

Causal regression models are most satisfactory when the variable to be forecast has a well-behaved relationship with a few easily identified external variables. They are much less satisfactory if the variable is influenced by a multitude of external variables or if the relationships that do exist are rather unclear. When this happens a better approach is to use time series models. These rely on using the past values of the variable to forecast its future values and obviously make sense if the data contain regular patterns or trends.

They also make sense if the past data can be regarded as being 'caused' by the multitude of influencing factors; in other words, if the variable's own past values can be seen as a sort of composite index for all the causal factors. Viewed in this way it would be no surprise if a variable's own past values turned out to be the best available 'explanatory' variable for its future values. Furthermore, the observations for this 'explanatory' variable are likely to be more up-to-date, more regular and collected on a more consistent basis than many conventional external variables.

The main shortcoming of time series models is that all the information required to forecast the future must somehow be contained in the historical data. Whether the series is viewed as a continuing pattern or as a composite index of causal variables, it is not likely that this information would be adequate to forecast very far ahead. Indeed, unless the data series is unusually stable most experts would rarely trust a time series forecast beyond about three months ahead.

Time series models are therefore most suitable when short-run forecasts are required at a fine level of detail. Weekly sales for one product line over a period of a month would be a typical example. Hence longer-run forecasts of the kind required by the example are not really appropriate subjects for this approach. Consequently, forecasts G, H and I, which are based on time series models, should be regarded with some suspicion. Causal models or even the non-quantitative methods discussed in chapter 2 would generally be preferable for longer-run forecasts.

Just as causal models must take care to be appropriate at a detailed level, so must time series models. If the data are thought to contain trends, cycles or seasonal movements then the selected model must be capable of handling such patterns. For example, forecast G uses single exponential smoothing which is really only appropriate for trend-free data. This is the reason for its implausible trend-free forecasts.

Forecast I was Holt's method of smoothing and forecast H uses a related method known as double exponential smoothing. Both these can handle a trend so are theoretically preferable to G for data which appear to contain a trend. However, neither can allow for seasonality. Thus if the data were thought to have a seasonal pattern these forecasts would also be inappropriate. In fact there is not much evidence of seasonality in the example data but the general principle still stands. A time series model must be correctly matched to its data.

Another approach to testing the theoretical plausibility of a forecasting model is to ask under what circumstances it would fail and whether such circumstances are very likely. All models take explicit account of only relatively few factors. Hence there is an implied assumption that all other factors will either remain roughly the same or else will cancel each other out. However, if these other factors do change in a systematic way the model structure will become inappropriate and it will begin to forecast badly. If it is possible to think of likely circumstances under which this could happen, the model is not very satisfactory.

The kind of structural change about which one should worry will vary from situation to situation. For example, forecast A is based on the continuation of a straight-line trend so it would never forecast a turning point. If a turning point or a change of trend occurs, that model will fail. The excellent fit observed in the forecast B regression depends entirely on the continuation of a high and steady inflation rate. If that rate continues it will forecast well; if not it will fail.

The better models, E and F, also have their problems. They depend entirely on the relationship between the increase in Gomme's sales and the increase in GDP (or consumers' expenditure). They make no allowance for stock building by retailers. Yet at the beginning of a down-turn in the economy one would expect retailers to de-stock, leaving a manufacturer such as Gomme with lower sales than the model would have predicted. The reverse error would be likely to occur at the beginning of an upswing.

Macroeconomic events such as nationwide de-stocking can of course be allowed for as long as somebody thinks of it; but this may not happen automatically. If not, an appropriate *ad hoc* adjustment has to be made. In the same way, forecasts may not take into account important events which are local to the company, such as the introduction of a new product or a big sales effort. Thus again it may well fall to the practical manager to realize that a vital new feature in the situation may have been overlooked.

Usually it takes a little time for the environment to change enough for a forecasting model to collapse. Consequently, forecasts of events close to the present are likely to be more reliable than forecasts of events further in the future. For example, in November 1982 the sales for 1982: 2 are already in the pipeline. About half those sales will have already occurred and a reasonable percentage of the rest will be in the order book. Hence that forecast should be fairly reliable. However, a great deal could change in the environment in a further year, so the forecast for 1983: 2 must be regarded as less reliable.

Some models, such as forecasts F and E, require inputs which are themselves forecasts. If these are not forecast very accurately or if they would not be available when needed then again the model can be expected to perform badly. In other words, a better fitting model may be worse overall if it requires inputs which cannot be forecast satisfactorily. For example, instead of relating Gomme's sales to GDP it might have been attractive to use consumers' expenditure on durable goods or even aggregate sales of domestic furniture. Unfortunately, reliable forecasts of these variables are not available, even though the relevant historical data exist and might fit well.

Many forecasters consider not needing forecast inputs to be a significant advantage of time series models. A model such as forecast H may be fairly naive but at least it does not require additional data sources to be used. By contrast the causal model for forecast F requires a forecast for real GDP growth and for price inflation before it can be used. Thus, even if the regression between actual GDP and actual inflation fits well, it will not be reliable if poor forecasts of those figures are used.

Input variables are not all forecast with equal accuracy. For example, the economy can be forecast very accurately and the MAD for the real GDP forecast a year ahead by the major forecasting services is about 1 per cent. However, as the economy is subdivided the accuracy of macroeconomic forecasts generally falls off. Thus expenditure on durable goods is likely to be less accurate than aggregate consumer expenditure. This in turn is likely to be less accurate than the forecast for total GDP. Since this pattern may continue as one approaches finer and finer levels of detail, it is obviously wise not to expect a MAD of 1 per cent at an industry or product level.

Prices are generally not forecast as accurately as GDP and furthermore there is a good deal of variation between different price series. Most macroeconomic forecasts offer several series, for both inputs and outputs, so it is important to make an appropriate choice. Assuming the Retail Price Index to be a reasonable average is not a good idea. This figure is substantially influenced by public sector monopoly prices and so does not reflect international competitive prices particularly well. Export prices are often regarded as a better choice, although it may be important to eliminate oil prices which in the UK account for about 10 per cent of exports.

The hardest variables to forecast are those which are based on calculating the net effect of a large number of positive and negative figures. Here the errors accumulate so that a forecast for the net figure is likely to be much worse than the forecasts for its individual components. Since the net may be small relative to the components, the percentage error may be even worse. For this reason one should expect forecasts of net figures, such as earnings or net cash flow, to be much less accurate than forecasts of sales. Some macroeconomic forecasts such as the balance of payments are likely to be inaccurate for the same reason.

Is the Forecasting Model Appropriate for the Job?

Before concluding this survey of forecast appraisal, it is worth pointing out that although our discussion has focused on accuracy, this is not the only consideration. The forecasting system must also be applicable to the situation in hand. Deciding whether it is or not usually has much more to do with traditional management skills than with forecasting techniques.

Different forecasting systems will obviously cost different amounts to implement. Generally there are three important components to the cost: development cost, data collection and storage costs, and computer processing time. All or any of these may be significant and the first and second have a reputation for being higher than anticipated! Thus it may be that a technically excellent forecasting system will have to be rejected if its cost is not justified by the expected benefits. If development and initial data collection are important there is an additional question of whether the system can be implemented quickly enough to be useful. Plenty of cases exist where over-ambitious forecasting systems have taken so long to install that they were obsolete before the task was finished.

Perhaps the most important question to ask about applying a

forecasting system is whether it can be properly integrated into the management decision process it is supposed to support. This is a large and difficult area which will be discussed more fully in chapter 7. However, at the very least, a good forecast must be adequate at a technical level and must suit the organization for which it is intended.

A technically satisfactory forecast must first of all be accurate enough for its purpose, which is why so much attention has been given to accuracy. In addition it must be designed to forecast for the correct period ahead. Even a completely accurate forecast for say, three months ahead, will be no use to a manager who has to work with a one-year lead time.

A different but closely related issue is responsiveness. Some models respond very rapidly to changing circumstances while others are much more sluggish. This is a totally predictable feature of different forecasting systems. In general, a rapid response is associated with rather erratic movements in the forecast whereas a sluggish response has the benefit of steadier, though possibly out-of-date, forecasts. Hence neither is necessarily best and the manager must judge the correct level of responsiveness for the situation.

Not all forecasting systems fit happily into the organization and make the expected contribution. Sometimes managers do not understand or do not believe the forecasts and tend to ignore them. Quite often they use them but not in the way that was intended. Frequently they use only those that suit their purpose and then only as ammunition in organizational battles. And of course, occasionally forecasts are used exactly as they are supposed to be used. Unfortunately this last possibility is most unlikely unless the manager responsible for the forecasting process has given serious thought to the human and organizational problems involved.

Conclusion

A wealthy professional forecaster was once asked how long it took his consultancy business to recover following a really bad forecast. His reply was that he had never made a really bad forecast. Sometimes actual results had turned out to be rather different from his forecasts but that was always because of exceptional circumstances or some other good reason. He went on to explain that researchers may be interested in a forecaster's track record but managers are more interested in his current forecasts. They know that objectively appraising forecasts is so difficult that it is usually a waste of time. They also know that the probability of making two really bad forecasts in succession is almost zero. Consequently after a bad one, the next forecast is almost certain to be good!

We hope that you can now see that such remarks are nonsense: appraising forecasts does require care and it is quite easy to misinterpret the results. Nevertheless the task is well within the capabilities of a non-specialist. In this chapter we explained that there are three steps:

1 Check the track record, because it does not follow from the law of averages that good forecasts generally follow from a bad track record.[3]
2 Check the plausibility of the forecaster's method. Implausible methods which appear to work are probably only identifying idiosyncrasies of the recent past. They may have a good track record but they can still forecast badly.
3 Check that the forecast is appropriate for its purpose. Otherwise, however accurate it may be, managers will ignore it.

Notes

1 The forecasts discussed in this chapter were made quite independently of the company, using only publicly available information. They do not in any way represent views which the company may have held.
2 This rule known as the sign test or the runs test is discussed in most statistics texts. See, for example, W.J. Conover, *Practical Nonparametric Statistics* (Wiley), pp. 112–42.
3 Readers who do not believe this may like to think about Woody Allen's wonderfully simple defence against airline highjacking. He suggests that you should always carry your own bomb because the probability of there being two bombs on the same plane is almost zero.

CHAPTER 7

Making a Forecasting System Work

Deciding which technique to use and assessing in advance how accurate it is likely to be are often seen as the only important (or, even, the only) parts of forecasting. The concept of a forecasting system suggests strongly that this is not so. The nine guidelines for forecasting design were described in chapter 1. They showed that a considerable amount of work had to be done before deciding upon a technique. In particular, the forecasts had to be integrated with the decision-making process which they were intended to serve. There is also work to be done after the technique has been decided upon and its accuracy assessed. This work is explained in guidelines 7 to 9. These stages concern incorporating judgements, implementing and monitoring respectively. They are equally as important as any of the other stages. Without them a forecasting system will fail. Nor should they be seen as separate topics. They are intimately linked with one another and with the other stages in the forecasting checklist. This chapter discusses the three topics in turn.

Incorporating Judgements into Forecasts

Inevitably, within an organization there will be people who, for good or bad reasons, disagree with the output of a forecasting system. If they are closely connected with the system as users of the forecasts, the matter is a serious one. They may be in a position to cause the system to fail. It is essential that they be brought inside the system and persuaded to see it as something to which they can contribute. They should see it as their system. User involvement is important throughout the design of a forecasting system. Stage 1, the analysis of the decision-taking process, should have ensured user involvement from the outset. It is important that it be continued through all stages of the design and when the forecasts are being used. Incorporating judgements into the forecasts is an excellent way of doing this.

If people are not permitted to influence the forecasts with their opinions, they may feel sufficiently disenchanted to hinder the system's success or at least not to put real effort into making it work. This is a rather negative reason for incorporating judgements into forecasts. The positive reason for incorporating judgements is that they probably contain information not obtainable elsewhere which will improve forecasting accuracy if it can be properly applied. The real value of judgements is that they can capture information of an instinctive nature, based on insight, information which it is difficult to articulate within the more usual data forms. For example, a company producing leisure software for microcomputers took the view that if their products were marketed in a particular way, then there would be a strong growth in sales. This view contradicted the hard quantitative data which indicated a falling off in sales in this area and an increasing number of companies in difficulty. The company built their sales forecasts around this judgement and the early indications are that they were right to do so. In many other industries where factors such as fashion, packaging and design play a significant part, judgemental information will be of great importance.

Of course judgemental information has its limitations. There are two main problems. The first is that it can be biased. Bias means being wrong in some particular and consistent way. Market research on behalf of some product is likely to be biased if it is solely housewives who are interviewed. Wives who work away from home will be omitted as well as all male consumers. The results of the research will reflect these omissions. A contrasting example of bias is that of an engineering (or financial or marketing) director and his forecasting judgements. They will be biased if he never considers issues other than those connected with engineering (or finance or marketing).

The second main problem is that information based on judgements can be inflexible (or conservative). Judgement tends to be reluctant to move far from the status quo. In a rising market the tendency is to underestimate; in a falling market the tendency is to overestimate. This is a regrettable defect since one would hope that judgement might be better able to forecast turning points than other techniques. The Further Reading list has references to surveys and other evidence about the effectiveness of judgemental information and associated difficulties.

How to Incorporate Judgements

The problems associated with information derived from judgements should not detract from its value but they should promote an attitude of caution with regard to its use. In spite of the problems, the importance of having some definite way of bringing judgements to bear on forecasts seems clear. How can it be done? There are two tasks to be accomplished. The first is to obtain some sort of consensus from what might be a long list of differing views. The second is to use this consensus to make adjustments to the forecasts which have already been derived by other means.

The first task draws on qualitative forecasting techniques. Two of them, structured groups and, especially the Delphi method, are generally helpful in this context. Obtaining a qualitative forecast by the Delphi method and bringing together judgements with a view to possible adjustments to quantitatively derived forecasts are similar exercises. However, there is a significant difference. The Delphi method requires participants to alter their opinions in coming to a forecast. When a statistical forecast is already on the table, participants may be reluctant to change their views. The element of competition which is inherent in Delphi may be more apparent when the aim is to adjust an existing forecast rather than to form a forecast from scratch. The participants may see themselves as part of a bargaining process rather than a scientific technique. Experience shows that a consensus is hard to achieve in these circumstances. This makes the next task, adjusting the forecasts, even more difficult.

There is no way to adjust the forecasts apart from a process of discussion and, eventually, agreement. The control on this process is that participants will be accountable for the decisions they make. The discussion must be minuted. At a later stage not only the forecasts themselves should be monitored, but also the adjustment of forecasts. If the minutes reveal that any participant in the adjustment process was insisting on a view which turned out to be incorrect, he or she will have to explain why. This may have a deterrent effect on game-playing. More importantly, a record will be built up over time. The people whose views are consistently correct will be evident from the record. Moreover, people whose judgements have consistently proved misguided, prejudiced or the product of vested interest will also be revealed. As time goes by the adjustment process should reflect more and more the track records of participants and less and less the strength with which they hold their opinion.

Of course the process is far from foolproof. Monitoring may deter some people from proffering their opinion; track records will mean little if there is a rapid turnover in participants; time is needed to build up track records; special cases will always be argued; most things can be explained away if one is clever enough. Nevertheless, the balance must be in favour of allowing judgements to be incorporated. Participation is better than non-participation. The alternative to allowing judgements to influence forecasts, with all the risks that entails, is to leave people who are intimately affected by the forecasts feeling that they are outside the system. Their positive input will not be available; a negative approach on their part may cause the system to fail.

Implementing the System

Suppose that the design of a forecasting system has progressed so far that there is available a technique capable of producing accurate forecasts which are in tune with the decision-making process. What happens next? Too often the answer is nothing. Many organizations and individuals pay lip service to the problem of implementation while in reality giving it scant attention. The procedure presented here suggests that the key to successful implementation is clear communication between those affected by the forecasts. Without clear communication it can prove very difficult for participants to agree on the problems, never mind the solutions.

The lack of communication can be seen in the polarized attitudes of the two major groups involved, the users and producers of the system. The former wonder how such theoretically minded experts can help practically minded managers; the latter wonder why so many people have yet to come out of the Stone Age. When such conflicting views exist the two sides are almost impossible to reconcile. The situation can be avoided by ensuring that users are concerned with the project from the outset. 'Us and them' feelings will then be minimized. The first stage of the design process, analysing the decision-making system, provides the ideal starting point for this co-operation.

How to Implement a System

Before a forecasting system can be implemented, it is therefore vital to involve the users. Otherwise, the steps suggested below can have little impact. Several research studies support the need for user involvement (see Further Reading, p. 195). In particular, it has been shown that involvement, in which the user feels that he or she has some influence on the design, is an important pre-requisite of success. With this proviso, the implementation stage should set out to answer four questions.

What are the problems? Forecasting experts tend either not to understand the users' problems or, if they do understand, to dismiss them as the product of a neanderthal mind. By adopting these positions much hard work is wasted and the system inevitably fails. A better approach is to find out what the problems really are by talking to the key people. Usually 'key people' means everyone even remotely affected by the forecasts. Managers who appear to be peripheral to a project often turn out to be remarkably imaginative in making their negative influence felt if their feathers have been ruffled because they have been excluded from the consultation. It is likely that the key people will come from a wide range of departments or functions: financial, marketing, operating management, purchasing, inventory control and many others depending upon the organization and the nature of the forecasting problem.

When talking to a potential user of the system it is important to adopt a neutral stance. It is likely to be the project leader who is conducting the interview. If, at this stage, he behaves like a salesman, the discussion may well polarize.

Sensitively conducted interviews of key users should reveal a range of problems over implementing the forecast. They may be rational, such as a lack of training for relevant clerical staff or an inability to understand the computer printouts on which the forecasts are to be issued; on the other hand, they may be less rational, such as a fear of increasing sophistication or a personality clash with one of the project leaders. Bringing these problems into the open will in itself help towards solving them.

Do all participants agree on the problems? Does it seem surprising that such agreement should be an issue? After all, a problem is a problem. In part, this question is answered merely by communicating the full range of problems to all participants. But there may be disagreements. For instance, there may be some doubt as to whether operators of the old manual system are the right people to operate the new system. Changes in budgets are another common source of dispute.

Continuing the consultations, perhaps supplemented by structured group meetings, the project leader hopes to obtain a consensus on all these issues. It is becoming more and more apparent that a forecasting expert needs skills in handling people just as much as quantitative ones. He should equip himself with these behavioural skills before embarking on the project. There are plenty of texts and courses to give him advice (see Further Reading, p. 195).

What are the possible solutions to the problems? The range of alternative solutions to the problems should come from the users. They are far more likely to make the system work if they know that the solutions are their own. The pressure will be on them to make their own solutions succeed.

The first step may be to persuade them that the problem is not insuperable and that there is benefit in trying to find an answer. The need for a new forecasting system should have been discussed when the project started, but it may be worthwhile going over the reasons once again to convince the users of the ill effects of staying with the status quo. Having obtained an agreement that the problems must be surmounted, the search for solutions can commence. Many will immediately have some ideas. Possibly brainstorming may be considered as a way of generating some more.

Can a consensus on an action plan be obtained? Throughout the implementation, the project leader has been walking a tightrope. At each stage he depends on his skill and the goodwill of others in order to make progress. This last question is probably the most difficult to answer. Vested interest, departmental pride, status, as well as genuinely held but conflicting views will all rise to the surface. There are techniques (beyond the scope of this text) to help a group leader to reach a consensus.

Even so, gaining a consensus in these conditions may prove too difficult a task for even the most skilful and well-equipped project leader. If a consensus is impossible, the next best thing is an experiment. Will the participants agree to an experiment? Of course the experiment would have to be for a limited period and include a provision for feedback. But it might provide the information and goodwill necessary for agreement at a later date; or, possibly, the experiment itself might be sufficient to overcome the inertia that tends to afflict most new ventures.

Example. An example of this exhaustive problem/solution approach to implementation comes from the banking world. A computerized forecasting system was to replace the previous group-discussion approach to planning new business activities. The implementation stage had been reached. Interviews and discussions between all the key people revealed a surprising range of problems, including:

Lack of self-confidence in using new techniques on the part of some users.
Concern over loss of control of forecasts.
Lack of faith in the producer department because of past failures.
The added management burden in dealing with computer output.

Some of these problems had already been provided for. The users were eventually convinced that meetings to incorporate judgements into forecasts allowed them control over forecasts as before, but with the advantage of the meetings being more soundly based on a statistical forecast. The other problems could not, however, be discarded. To cope with the added management burden, the producers of the forecasts had to agree to a substantial simplification of the printout and a tailoring of the output to individual users' needs. The users' lack of confidence both in themselves and the producers proved yet more difficult to solve. Eventually a series of experiments was agreed. The system would be introduced in one department at a time. Meanwhile the other departments would continue to operate the manual system. A strict feedback procedure would allow the users to learn from the experience of others and to make necessary alterations as the implementation proceeded. As a result implementation was a lengthy process (and emotionally draining for the project leader) but it led to an end product that was worth waiting for – a forecasting system that worked.

   Of course all situations differ and there is a need for flexibility on all sides. One factor, however, is always a great bonus: this is when one of the users is sufficiently convinced of the need for a new system or sufficiently enthusiastic about the new technology and techniques to take on a leadership role. If the users are being motivated by one of their own side rather than by an expert with whom they seem to have little contact, many of the difficulties simply do not arise. This factor is now seen as increasingly important in the implementation of new technology, whether related to forecasting or not. Indeed, all the ideas suggested in this section go far beyond the implementation of forecasting systems. They apply to the implementation of any new methods, techniques or practices.

Monitoring Performance

Surveys show that few organizations monitor the performance of their forecasting systems. This may seem surprising but it is perfectly consistent with an approach which fails to see forecasting as a system. A non-systematic view sees forecasting as a technique which provides forecasts; a systematic view sees forecasting as a wide-ranging and dynamic process which takes in all the nine guidelines and which is continually being adjusted. The ninth and final stage is monitoring – the regular evaluation of the health of the system.

The best monitoring goes further than simple assessment and the allocation of praise or blame. It provides the information on which improvements in the system can be based. The evidence can show not just how accurate the forecasts have been, but when and why the forecasts have been good or bad.

At what time periods were the forecasting errors unacceptably high?

Does the system fail to capture properly the seasonal effect, or business cycles, or changes in the economic environment?

Have turning points in the forecast variable been missed?

Have the forecasts been made acceptable only by the incorporation of judgements?

Or have they been made unacceptable only because of the incorporation of judgements?

Were the statistics and the judgements equally disastrous?

Whose judgements have proved to be sound and whose unsound?

Questions such as these should be asked, and answered, regularly. The emphasis is on regularity. Monitoring should not be a simple reaction to some disaster or near-disaster; nor should it be an occasional lightning audit to catch people out. Rather, it should be a continual flow of information.

How to Monitor Performance

Monitoring will, therefore, stem from regular reports comparing the actual data as they become known with the forecasts. The reports will include purely statistical measures of accuracy, similar to those used in assessing the accuracy of techniques. Thus the mean absolute deviation (MAD) and mean square error (MSE) will be used to indicate the average level of accuracy over the time period in question. Beyond this, general summary information is required, possibly on a management-by-exception basis. Times of exceptional accuracy or inaccuracy should be reported with, where possible, reasons for the deviation. For instance, the report might say that the third-quarter forecasts were inaccurate, just as they were in the last two years; or, that the third-quarter forecasts were inaccurate for the first time because of the special circumstance of, say, a strike.

If the system allows for forecasts to be altered to reflect judgements then, in addition to these frequent monitoring reports, there must also be less regular reports assessing the performance of the 'judges'. Track records must be compiled showing which judges have been accurate and which inaccurate. Even if a particular judge's views have not been included so far, they may be at some time in the future and it will be useful to have his or her track record to hand.

Amongst all this statistical data it is worth remembering that it is not always the forecasts which are closest to the actual data that are the best. This paradox comes about as follows. In one important sense, the best forecasts are those that have credibility with the users. If they have credibility then notice will be taken of them and management action will follow. This action may cause the originally recorded forecasts to appear inaccurate. Their true accuracy can, of course, never be known because conditions have changed (by the taking of management action). Accordingly, a comprehensive monitoring system should go beyond numerical data and consider perceptions of value and success. In other words, the users will be questioned from time to time and their opinions of the strengths and weaknesses of the system collected. It may be that a moderately accurate but functioning system is preferable to a highly accurate but never used system.

For example, the senior management of a manufacturing company could not understand why production planning decisions were so poor. A check on the forecasting system which supported the decisions revealed that the forecasts were highly accurate. A check on the way decisions were made uncovered the surprising information that the forecasts were never used by the production planners. They used their own 'seat of the pants' judgements as forecasts. The reason turned out to be that the system had not been properly implemented. Liaison between producers and users had been very poor and the computer-based system had never been explained to those who were to receive the output. As a result the planners felt threatened and isolated by the system and ignored it. If less effort had been channelled into obtaining high levels of accuracy and more into making sure users knew what to do with the forecasts, the overall benefits to the organization would have been considerable.

In this example the failure of the forecasting system naturally gave cause for concern. Just as disturbing must have been the fact that no-one was aware of its failure until the evidence of the bad decisions started to roll in. Such poor communication is a surprisingly frequent occurrence. In more organizations than would wish to acknowledge it, producers and users of forecasting systems (or other management aids) hold diametrically opposed views about the success or failure of the project. The producers think it a success; the users think it a failure. The producers do not go to talk to the users because they think all is fine; the users think the non-appearance of the producers is because they are too ashamed. The users do not go to talk to the producers because they feel they lack the competence to complain and do not wish to get sucked into a discussion of the technicalities of forecasting; the producers think the non-appearance of the users is because they are too busy using the excellent system. If the two sides do meet the users are too polite to say what they say between themselves; the producers think the users' faint praise is because their success is grudged. Such situations reinforce the view that survey checks conducted by an independent body a short while after a system has become operational are a necessity, not a luxury.

In summary, there is nothing very sophisticated about the monitoring of forecasting performance. Its essentials are the recording of comprehensive data, both quantitative and qualitative, together with a willingness to face facts and act upon them. Perhaps this is why so few organizations monitor their forecasts. The excitement of forecasting, such as it is, lies in the techniques. There is no excitement in tedious and continuing data evaluations and therefore, some might think, monitoring must be an unimportant part of the process.

Conclusion

The topics covered in this chapter – the incorporation of judgement, implementation and monitoring – are often given too little attention within the context of forecasting; this is generally true in books, courses, research or the activities of organizations. A moment's thought demonstrates that this is an error. If a forecasting technique is wrongly applied, good monitoring will permit it to be adjusted speedily; the situation can be retrieved. If judgements, implementation or monitoring are badly done or ignored, communication between producers and users will probably disappear and it will be virtually impossible to retrieve the situation. Statistical mistakes can lose a battle; management mistakes can lose the war.

Why should these issues be held in such low regard? Perhaps the answer lies in the widespread attitude which says that a manager needs to be taught statistical methods but that the handling of judgements, implementation and monitoring are matters of instinct which all good managers have. These are undoubtedly management skills, but whether they are instinctive is another matter. Whatever the reason, the effect of this inattention is almost certainly a stream of failed forecasting systems.

How can the situation be corrected? A different attitude on the part of all concerned would certainly help, but attitudes are notoriously hard to change. A long-term, yet realistic approach calls for more information. Comparatively little is known about these management issues, although recently more has been published. Much of this concerns management science techniques in general rather than forecasting in particular. Nevertheless, it is still the case that if reports and research on the management aspects of forecasting systems were as plentiful as those on the technical aspects, a great improvement could be anticipated.

CHAPTER 8

Using Microcomputer Spreadsheet Packages in Forecasting

A great deal of business forecasting begins with a sales forecast which is then used to calculate forecast values of a mass of other variables. Wages, material costs, depreciation, tax, stock levels, earnings and cash flow are all examples. Frequently these other variables will be highly sensitive to errors in the sales forecast. Hence it will usually be necessary to try alternative sales values to see what difference they would make. And it is not only a wrong sales forecast that can make the other figures go wrong. A whole variety of other inputs, in particular unit costs and prices, are also needed, so it will be necessary to try out alternative assumptions for those forecasts as well.

In recent years, the process of putting all the forecasts together and checking the consequences of different assumptions has been revolutionized by the advent of microcomputers. This is predominantly because of spreadsheet programs such as Visicalc, Multiplan and Lotus 1–2–3 which are ideally suited to this task.

These ingenious programs allow the computer to behave rather like an enormous sheet of traditional multi-column analysis paper; hence the name spreadsheet. On the sheet, text or numbers can be written in the many available cells as easily as they can on paper. In addition, and quite unlike paper, formulae can be written which automatically carry out calculations using the other entries in the sheet. This means that whenever any of those other entries are changed the whole sheet can easily be recalculated.

When testing the consequences of different forecasting assumptions, the benefits of such a program are enormous. The appropriate formulae have to be worked out and entered into the sheet only once. After that it is a simple matter to plug in as many alternative assumptions as required. For each one the computer will carry out all the tedious calculations and print out the final answer. However, to use these programs effectively requires a certain amount of skill. The object of this chapter is to illustrate an approach and, at the same time, to point out some of the pitfalls and explain a few tricks of the trade.

As far as possible no specific spreadsheet program will be assumed because most of the basic principles are the same for all of them. In the few cases where there are important differences this will be pointed out. Where examples must be completely specific the conventions used in Lotus 1–2–3 will be adopted. However, it needs to be stressed that the majority of the chapter is quite general and much of it even applies to pencil and paper solutions.

The basic idea is to start with a list of assumptions – variables which have already been forecast using the methods described elsewhere in this book. These assumptions then have to be fed into the model in such a way that the value of all other variables can be calculated. In the technical jargon the variables that have to be forecast before the model can be used are known as exogenous variables because they are external to the model. By contrast variables that are calculated within the model are known as endogenous variables. The process of trying out different values for the exogenous variables to see what impact they have on the value of the endogenous variables is known as sensitivity analysis. In order to illustrate spreadsheet modelling and sensitivity analysis an example will be considered which requires some cash flow forecasts to be made.

Watlington Limited has approached its bank requesting an increase in its overdraft limit to £150,000. The current overdraft is £51,000 and the current limit is £100,000. The company has been a good customer of the bank for five years and has a successful record of growth and profitability. Consequently the bank will probably view the request favourably. Nevertheless, it will need to make some cash flow forecasts to check that the increased limit is appropriate.

The latest accounts of the company are shown in table 8.1 and, at least as a starting point, it can be assumed that sales will continue to grow at 15 per cent per annum. The other accounting relationships can also be assumed to remain more or less as they were in 1983 and 1984. The only exception is the stock level, which was at an abnormally low level in 1984. A more typical level would have been £359,000 rather than £280,000. Indeed the company's main justification for the overdraft increase is to finance the restoration of stock levels. However, another significant need for cash is the planned expenditure on fixed assets. In order to maintain enough operating capacity to cope with sales growth the company is planning to spend £500,000 a year in 1985 and in 1986.

Forecasting bank overdraft is quite difficult because it cannot be forecast in isolation. Instead it must be viewed as a consequence of the many other factors interacting with each other in the business. For example, Watlington will need money to rebuild stocks and purchase additional fixed assets. Some of this expenditure will be covered by profit and no doubt some more can be found by increasing creditors. However, until the amount of these, and other, sources and uses of finance are known it is impossible to calculate the size of the gap to be filled by the overdraft. Consequently, in order to forecast overdraft, it is first necessary to forecast all the other elements in the profit and loss account and balance sheet.

In practical terms, what has to be done is to add forecasts for 1985 and 1986 alongside the actuals already given in table 8.1 for 1983 and 1984. The easiest way is to work systematically through the profit and loss account and the balance sheet.

Table 8.1   Profit and loss accounts and balance sheets for Watlington Limited for 1983 and 1984

PROFIT AND LOSS ACCOUNTS (£000)

	1983	1984
Sales	2500	2875
Cost of goods sold	1625	1869
Gross profit	875	1006
Depreciation	206	237
Interest paid	4	7
Other costs	500	575
	710	819
Profit before tax	165	187
Taxation	68	77
	97	110
Dividend	50	50
Retained profit	47	60

BALANCE SHEETS (£000)

	1983	1984
Fixed assets at cost	1102	1267
Accumulated depreciation	490	563
Net fixed assets	612	704

Table 8.1 *cont.*

Stock	312	280
Debtors	185	213
Cash	20	23
Current assets	517	516
Total assets	1129	1220
Ordinary shares	600	600
Reserves	130	190
Shareholders' equity	730	790
Bank overdraft	62	51
Creditors	233	268
Tax due	54	61
Dividend due	50	50
Current liabilities	399	430
Liabilities and equity	1129	1220

Forecasting the Elements of the Profit and Loss Account

Sales is, of course, the first value to be forecast. It is an exogenous variable and, at least for the time being, can be assumed to be growing steadily at 15 per cent per year. Consequently, the most recent figure of £2,875,000 can be expected to grow to £3,306,000 in 1985 and £3,802,000 in 1986.

In sensitivity analysis it is frequently convenient to separate inflation from sales volume growth. This is because some variables, such as production capacity, will depend on sales volume while others, such as debtors, are more likely to depend on sales value. For instance, it might be that the sales growth of 15 per cent was based on assuming 10 per cent for inflation and 5 per cent for volume growth.

The cost of goods sold and other costs are the next variables to forecast. For Watlington they appear to maintain a very stable percentage of sales. In fact the cost of goods sold is about 65 per cent of sales and 'other costs' is about 20 per cent of sales. It is therefore reasonable to assume that the cost of goods sold will be £2,149,000 in 1985 and £2,471,000 in 1986 while other costs will be £661,000 in 1985 and £760,000 in 1986.

In practice the approach of using a simple percentage may work quite well, but its realism in any particular case is an empirical question and should not be taken for granted. Often, breaking the costs down into more detail will be helpful; for example, separating labour from material. Also, more reliable forecasts will often result from explicitly including a fixed element in costs.

Under inflationary conditions it is extremely easy to underestimate the importance of fixed costs. This arises because a regression line relating sales to costs will frequently fit well and have only a small constant term in the regression equation. This appears to indicate firstly, that the regression equation provides a reliable forecasting relationship and secondly that fixed costs are not too important. Unfortunately, both conclusions are frequently wrong.

This paradoxical result occurs because under inflationary conditions both costs and selling prices drift upwards. Hence the relationship between sales and costs changes from year to year. If costs and prices all increase at roughly the same rate the successive cost curves will remain more or less parallel[1] and the situation will be approximately as illustrated in figure 8.1. If different inflation rates are involved the slopes as well as the levels of the cost curves will vary from year to year.

Historical values of sales and costs will typically have been generated by sales increasing while the cost curve was moving upwards. Consequently they will form a line, rather like the dots in figure 8.1, which bears no relation to any actual cost curve. Thus the observed regression line will have a lower intercept than the actual fixed cost and a steeper slope than the actual variable cost. Furthermore, the regression fit will typically be much better than would have been the case in the absence of inflation. This is because the inflation rate enters both sides of the regression equation and in practice the effect can be quite significant. For example, given 10 to 15 years of annual data and an inflation rate of about 10 per cent, it is quite possible to observe very high R squared values when there is only a weak relationship between the underlying variables.

The reasons why such a model might give very poor forecasts should now be clear. The relationship is mis-specified and does not correctly distinguish between inflation and sales volume growth. If either behaves unusually the forecast will be incorrect. For example, if inflation was expected to fall to zero between 1985 and 1986 the true

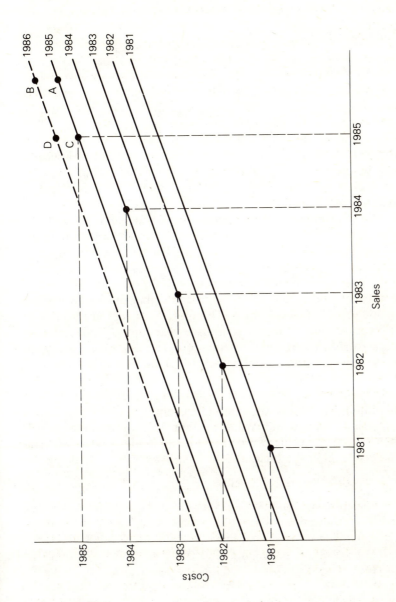

Figure 8.1 An upward drift in sales and costs caused by inflation.

cost curve would remain the same for both years. Nevertheless the regression line would assume a parallel movement and would forecast costs at, say, point B in figure 8.1. Consequently, a substantial error would arise when the actual value was subsequently observed at point A.

A similar problem arises if the sales volume growth is unusual, even if the inflation rate takes its average value. For example, suppose the sales volume was forecast to decline so that the 1986 value was expected to be about the same as the 1985 value. The regression line would of course predict unchanged costs because of the unchanged sales values so it would forecast point C. However, inflation would raise the 1986 cost curve above the 1985 level so the forecast would turn out to be an underestimate of the actual cost. It would be nearer to point D.

The solution to this problem is quite simple and requires no more than adjusting sales and costs by an appropriate inflation index before calculating the regression equation. The result will then relate sales and costs in prices of the index base year and give a much better model of the underlying relationship.

The only inconvenience of this approach is that the forecasts have to be made using base-year prices. Therefore it is necessary to convert a sales forecast from actual prices to base-year prices. Then costs can be forecast using the regression equation. The resulting cost figure will be in base-year prices, so the final step requires it to be converted back to actual prices.

The technique is more straightforward than it may sound and can be illustrated by means of a simple example. Table 8.2 shows historical data for sales and costs, together with a price index which has been used to calculate inflation-adjusted sales and costs. The regression line relating adjusted costs to adjusted sales is given by[2].

$$\text{cost} = 826 + 0.269 \times \text{sales} \qquad R \text{ squared} = 0.66$$

If the sales forecast for 1986 is £15m and the price index forecast is 459, it follows that sales in base-year prices would be 100 × £15m/459 = £3,268,000. The implied cost level is 826 + 0.269 × £3,268,000 = £1,705,000 at base-year prices or £1,705,000 × 459/100 = £7,826,000 at 1986 prices.

Depreciation is the next profit and loss account expense to be calculated; with the available information this is a difficult task. To a large extent the figure will be determined by assets already on the books but the detailed calculation would require knowledge of information which is

Table 8.2 Sales and costs under inflation

Year	Actual sales	Actual costs	Price index	Adjusted sales	Adjusted costs
1970	1500	1280	100	1500	1280
1971	1733	1496	110	1575	1360
1972	1997	1295	121	1650	1070
1973	2314	1882	133	1740	1415
1974	2657	1767	146	1820	1210
1975	3075	2101	161	1910	1305
1976	3559	2443	177	2010	1380
1977	4115	2516	195	2110	1290
1978	4751	3338	214	2220	1560
1979	5499	3540	236	2330	1500
1980	6346	3950	259	2450	1525
1981	7325	4560	285	2570	1600
1982	8447	4679	314	2690	1490
1983	9764	5037	345	2830	1460
1984	11286	6156	380	2970	1620
1985	13042	7211	418	3120	1725

not available: book value, age, depreciation policy and so forth. To a lesser extent the depreciation charge will be affected by new assets acquired during the forecast period. This figure is known for Watlington but insufficient detail is known about the company's depreciation policy. In order to make any further progress it is necessary to make some assumptions.

One approach which leads to particularly convenient results requires just two further assumptions. The first is that the average life (although not necessarily the average age) of Watlington's assets is remaining roughly constant. The second assumption is that over recent years their fixed asset investment has been growing at a steady annual rate.[3] If both these assumptions are satisfied it follows, under straight-line or reducing-balance depreciation, that the ratio of the depreciation charge to the year-end net book value of fixed assets will remain roughly constant.

This ratio of depreciation charged to net book value for Watlington is 33.66 per cent in both 1983 and 1984, so it seems reasonable to assume that the same value might hold for 1985 and 1986. In fact it is possible to prove that this cannot be absolutely correct. Nevertheless, it provides a good enough approximation and enables the depreciation charge to be calculated. There is, however, one minor problem to be overcome.

The equation for depreciation is

$$\text{Depn}_{85} = 0.3366 \times \text{NFA}_{85}$$

and the equation for net fixed assets is

$$\text{NFA}_{85} = \text{NFA}_{84} + \text{FA acquisition}_{85} - \text{Depn}_{85}$$

Hence there is a simultaneous relationship between depreciation and net fixed assets. It is not particularly difficult to solve and, if the first formula is substituted into the second, both figures are easily calculated. Net fixed assets has to be £901,000 and depreciation £303,000. In the same way the equivalent figures for 1986 work out to be £1,048,000 and £353,000.

Unfortunately, handling simultaneous equations by substitution is rather inconvenient for sensitivity analysis. If spreadsheet software is being used, there is a much easier approach. The simultaneous nature of the relationship is completely ignored and instead the recalculate key is pressed a few times. This may seem too simple to be true but the method usually works and is illustrated for the current problem in table 8.3.

Table 8.3   The recalculation method of solving simultaneous equations

			Recalculation number					
	A B	0	1	2	3	4	5	6
1	Depn = 0.3366 * B2	0	405	269	315	299	305	303
2	NFA = 1204 − B1	1204	799	935	889	905	899	901

The left-hand part of table 8.3 shows the two relevant lines of the spreadsheet model and the right-hand part shows the result of the successive recalculations. When the formulae are first entered into the computer the displayed values are completely wrong but after six recalculations they have changed enough to be roughly correct. A sufficient number of additional recalculations will improve the accuracy to any desired degree. If you have access to a microcomputer with a spreadsheet program it would be a good idea to try this out for yourself because the simplicity of the method can be hard to believe until you have tried it.

Solving simultaneous equations in a forecasting model by successive recalculation does not always work. Sometimes, instead of the successive calculations converging to a correct answer, they will diverge with each calculation moving further and further away from the correct answer. When this happens it is usually very obvious and in practice it is difficult to confuse convergence and divergence.

The simplicity of the method is seen even more clearly if the model is extended as shown in table 8.4. This time the two years are both calculated at once so it is very easy to carry out sensitivity analysis by altering the planned acquisition in 1985 and 1986.

If this model is entered in a real spreadsheet program it will show the wrong answer at first. Thereafter, with each successive recalculation the displayed numbers change less and less as the solution is approached. After about ten recalculations the correct values are displayed. When this point is reached, a worthwhile exercise is to change the fixed asset acquisition shown in cells C4 and D4 from 500 to 250. Then recalculate a few more times and watch all the values change until the model finds the new solution.

Table 8.4   The fixed asset and depreciation formulae

	A	B	C	D
1	Year	1984	1985	1986
2	Depreciation	237	+C3*B5	+D3*B5
3	NFA	704	+B3+C4−C2	+C3+D4−D2
4	Acquisition	329	500	500
5	Depn/NFA	+B2/B3	+C2/C3	+D2/D3

The technique of solving simultaneous equations by repeated recalculation is invaluable in forecasting models because it avoids the need for tedious and error-prone algebraic substitution. However, most spreadsheet programs treat it, quite rightly, as a dangerous practice. Consequently they often discourage its use. The concern is that if recalculation is carried out too few times the result will give a wrong answer which, once printed, would be almost impossible to detect.

The interest charge, like depreciation, involves a simultaneous relationship. Interest depends on the level of debt outstanding during the year. But the level of debt will depend on whether or not the company has been profitable which itself depends on the interest charge. However, unlike depreciation, the relationships linking interest and debt will be quite complicated since they have to take account of tax and other forms of finance. Even for Watlington they would be quite difficult to solve without a computer.

Fortunately, the method of repeated recalculation can be used again so at this stage it is only necessary to specify the appropriate formulae. The actual recalculations to find the appropriate values can be left until the whole model has been set up.

If it is assumed that the overdraft increases or decreases steadily throughout the year, then the average overdraft level can be used as the basis for calculating interest. Assume for convenience that Watlington had no overdraft at the end of 1982. Hence the average debts in 1983 and 1984 would have been £31,000 and £57,000 respectively, so the effective interest rate for those years was between 12 and 13 per cent. For simplicity assume that 12 per cent is thought to be an appropriate rate to use for 1985 and 1986. It then follows that the interest charge will be 12 per cent of the average of the opening and closing debt levels. The method of forecasting these debt levels will be considered in due course when we come to forecast the balance sheet.

The tax charge is the next figure in the profit and loss account and in many cases it will be one of the most difficult to forecast. The simplest approach is to calculate it as a percentage of profit before tax using either a forecast or a historical average for the percentage. For example, Watlington's tax as a percentage of profit before tax is about 41 per cent in both 1983 and 1984 so that figure might be appropriate for use in 1985 and 1986. Unfortunately, even if this figure is realistic, the actual tax charge cannot be calculated because the interest and hence the profit before tax are not known. Thus, once again, all that can be done is to specify the formula and leave the actual calculation until later.

Using a simple percentage of profit does not, of course, reflect the intricacies of the British tax system so it should not be relied upon too much. In particular it will take no account of any of the following factors:

1 Differences between capital allowances and reported depreciation.

2 Stock relief in those years when it applied.

3 Unrelieved advanced corporation tax.

4 Complications caused by group or consortium relief.

5 Complications caused by overseas tax.

6 Changing accounting practice in relation to deferred tax.

In most cases it would be inappropriate to take account of all these features of the tax system in a spreadsheet model. On the other hand, it is not usually very difficult to make some adjustment for capital allowances, stock relief, and advanced corporation tax. Including these features of the tax system can make a worthwhile improvement to the forecasting model. Nevertheless, for the sake of simplicity, they will not be taken into account for Watlington.

Dividend is the last profit and loss account charge that has to be calculated. It will probably be determined by management in the light of the overall picture shown by the profit and loss account and balance sheet. One option, therefore, is to treat it as exogenous, trying a number of different values to see which makes the most sense. However, managers generally avoid cutting the dividend whenever possible and will often increase it only in line with their long-run expectations of profit rather than to reflect a single good year. Thus some sort of heavily damped response to profit will often work quite well. For example, a fixed percentage of accumulated retained profit may be satisfactory particularly if it is somehow made 'sticky' in a downward direction.

In the case of Watlington it will be assumed, at least initially, that dividends will be held at their 1986 level of £50,000. When the whole forecast is completed this figure may turn out to be unrealistic in which case it can be revised either upwards or downwards.

Forecasting the Elements of the Balance Sheet

Net fixed assets have already been calculated in order to calculate the depreciation charge. However, in addition to net fixed assets, it may be necessary to forecast separately fixed assets at cost and accumulated depreciation. This may be quite difficult, and is frequently not necessary, but one approach would be to assume that the ratio of net fixed assets to fixed assets at cost remains roughly constant. In Watlington this ratio expressed as a percentage was 55.5 per cent in both 1983 and 1984 so the assumption seems reasonable. Thus fixed assets at cost would be forecast as £1,579,000 in 1985 and £1,863,000 in 1986. By subtracting the appropriate net fixed asset figures this gives accumulated depreciation of £660,000 in 1985 and £788,000 in 1986.

Stock, the next item on the balance sheet, is usually forecast in terms of the number of days of stock needed at the year end. This may be calculated on the basis of sales or cost of goods sold. In the case of Watlington the ratio of cost of goods sold to sales had already been assumed to be constant, so the choice is immaterial. However, in general the cost of goods sold is to be preferred. For Watlington the relevant figures are 70 days in 1983 and 55 days in 1984.

It was mentioned earlier that the low figure in 1984 was abnormal and had stock been at the planned level of £359,000 the stock days would have been 70. Thus 70 days looks like a sensible figure on which to base the forecast. Cost of goods sold has already been forecast as £2,150,000 in 1985 and £2,472,000 in 1986 so it follows that stock can be forecast as $2,150 \times 70/365 = £412,000$ in 1985 and $2,472,000 \times 70/365 = £474,000$ in 1986.

One problem that can arise with stock forecasts, although not for Watlington, is rapid-growth bias. It occurs when a company is growing (or declining) quite rapidly so that comparing its year-end stock level with its sales for the whole year gives a false relationship. So long as the same rate of growth (or decline) continues throughout the forecast period the consequences will not be too serious. However, if stock days are calculated during a period of high growth while the forecast is for a period of lower growth, the forecast stock level is likely to overshoot. Conversely, if growth is higher for the forecast period than it has been historically, the stock forecast is likely to undershoot. Furthermore these errors will occur even though the cost of goods sold may have been forecast with complete accuracy.

As a rough guide, some correction is generally advisable if the growth rate is either consistently above 20 per cent or else if it changes a great deal from year to year. Fortunately the correction is not particularly difficult, but there are two alternative approaches. These can be most easily understood by reference to figure 8.2.

The figure shows a graph for sales and stock during the period. The stock line is simply the presumed stock level on each day of the year. Hence the stock levels published in the balance sheet would be those at the beginning and end of the year, in other words, the points marked on the stock line as I_{t-1} and I_t.

The sales line is not quite so easy to interpret because it shows the annual rate of sales not the level of sales. To calculate the level from the rate it is necessary to multiply the rate by the time for which it applies. If many different rates apply during the year, then it is necessary to multiply each rate by the time for which it applied and add them all together. In terms of figure 8.2 this is equivalent to

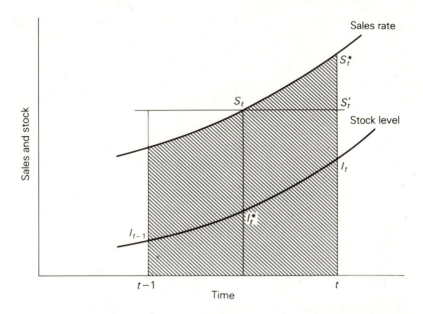

Figure 8.2   A graph of sales and stock to illustrate rapid growth bias.

saying that total sales for the year is given by the shaded area under the sales graph between dates $t - 1$ and t.

Different sales graphs could, of course, have the same area underneath them. For example, both the curve and the horizontal line through S_t cover the same area. Consequently, if only the figure for total sales is known (i.e. the area under the curve) it is impossible to identify the shape of the graph which existed during the period. This is the basic problem behind rapid-growth bias.

If stock days are calculated by relating the closing balance sheet stock figure to the profit and loss account sales figure, then one is relating I_t to S_t. So long as the sales graph is horizontal this makes sense. The year-end rate of sales would be S'_t which is the same as S_t. However it does not make sense if the graph is rising rapidly because then the year-end rate of sales would be S^*_t and the ratio of I_t to S_t would overestimate the true relationship.

There are two different solutions to the problem. One is to calculate a mid-year stock level (I^*_t) which is comparable to S_t. The other is to calculate the year-end rate of sales (S^*_t) which is comparable to I_t. The former is simpler and is usually carried out by averaging I_t and I_{t-1}

to provide an estimate of I^*_t. Stock days can then be calculated using I^*_t/S_t. If this ratio is used in forecasting it is important to remember that it will predict the mid-year and not the year-end stock level. A further adjustment to calculate the year-end stock level must be carried out using the formula:

$$I_{t+1} = 2I^*_{t+1} - I_t$$

This method, using average stock, will work reasonably well if the relationship between sales and stock is 'well behaved' like the one shown in figure 8.2. On the other hand, it will not work so well if:

1 Stock and sales are not growing parallel.
2 The growth of stock is significantly non-linear.
3 There is reason to believe that the two stock figures are not comparable.
4 The more recent stock figure is thought to be more typical of the current stock policy.

If any of these difficulties apply then the second approach will generally be better. Instead of looking at the mid-year position by calculating I^*_t, one looks at the year-end position by estimating S^*_t and calculating I_t/S^*_t. The main difficulty is selecting an appropriate growth path from the infinite number of possibilities – one that leads to relatively simple results and assumes continuous compound growth throughout the year. Under this assumption the year-end rate of sales can be calculated from the following formula where g is the continuous compound growth rate.

$$S^*_t = gS_t/(1 - e^{-g})$$

Unfortunately there is no easy way of observing the appropriate growth rate from published information. Interim or quarterly results may give some clues and so may recent year-to-year growth rates. However, quite often it comes to using an educated guess.

As with the average stock method some adjustment is necessary when using the adjusted stock days figure for forecasting. This time the ratio can be used to forecast I^*_{t+1} from which I_{t+1} can be calculated but it is probably better to forecast I_{t+1} directly. This requires the formula to be used to calculate the year-end sales rate (S^*_{t+1}) from the forecast of S_{t+1}. Then S^*_{t+1} can be used to forecast I_{t+1}.

Debtors and creditors can be forecast using essentially the same method as that used for stock. An estimate is made of the year-end debtor or creditor days and this is used to make a forecast. As with stock days, there are a number of options for the precise definition of debtor and creditor days. For example, it would usually be better to use sales or even credit sales rather than cost of goods sold in the figure for debtor days. On the other hand, cost of goods sold or some other aggregate of costs might work better for creditor days. In either case it may be helpful to separate trade from non-trade debtors and creditors. However, all these questions are empirical because the most important consideration is to find the best-fitting relationship.

In the case of Watlington, debtor days and creditor days both appear to be very stable. Debtors represent 27 days of sales and creditors represent 34 days of sales. If these figures are used to forecast debtors and creditors it gives, for debtors, $3,306,000 \times 27/365$ = £245,000 in 1985 and $3,802,000 \times 27/365$ = £281,000 in 1986. For creditors the figures are $3,306,000 \times 34/365$ = £308,000 in 1985 and $3,802,000 \times 34/365$ = £354,000 in 1986.

The problem of rapid-growth bias applies as much to debtors and creditors as it does to stock. Indeed it applies whenever an income statement figure is compared with a balance sheet figure. However Watlington's consistent but modest growth rate means that the effect will be slight and no correction is necessary.

Cash is the next balance sheet figure to be forecast and to do this it is useful to distinguish between two different components of the cash balance. The first is the working capital element which is necessary to pay bills and cope with emergencies. This will generally relate to the level of activity and naturally varies a good deal from business to business. For example, retailers or banks need quite substantial cash balances whereas manufacturers who operate on credit need much less.

The second element is the temporary investment in cash which results as a consequence of all other activities rather than representing a specific need. In practice it is not easy to tell how much cash is in each category. Thus, when forecasting, the distinction between working capital cash, investment cash, bank overdraft and even loans can become blurred.

If cash is assumed to be needed for working capital then it can be forecast like stock, debtors or creditors in terms of days' sales. Watlington, for example, has a fairly consistent figure of 2.9 days so the cash need could be forecast as $2.9 \times 3,306,000/365$ = £26,000 in 1985, and $2.9 \times 3,802,000/365$ = £30,000 in 1986. Alternatively, if the cash balance is thought to be a consequence of everything else it is best not even to attempt a forecast. Instead it should be aggregated with overdraft and treated as the figure which balances the books. This will be explained further below when forecasting the debt level is discussed.

The tax liability will often be as difficult to forecast as the tax charge. This is because the charge and the liability are so closely related. The rules determining the date for tax payments are quite specific so an accurate forecast of the charge should imply an accurate forecast of the liability. On the other hand, an incorrect forecast of the charge is likely to lead directly to an incorrect forecast of the liability.

A simple but very rough approach is to assume that the tax due is some percentage of the tax charge. For example, in Watlington in 1983 and 1984 this percentage was between 78 per cent and 80 per cent so one could take 80 per cent of the tax charge as a rough way of forecasting the amount of tax due. Obviously this approach is very approximate, but it may provide a satisfactory starting point from which sensitivity analysis can subsequently be carried out.

Dividend liability is frequently just the final dividend because the interim dividend will have been paid out before the year end. If the interim is zero, then of course the dividend liability will be the same as the dividend charged in the profit and loss account. This appears to be the case for Watlington. However, if a company usually pays an interim dividend, an appropriate amount must be deducted from the charge to give the correct year-end liability. As with tax due, an easy approach is to use a reasonable percentage of the proposed dividend as the dividend liability.

Shareholders' equity has two components – shares and reserves. In a simple model both are best handled in a simple way. Shares can be treated as exogenous with an appropriate *ad hoc* adjustment being made when the debt/equity ratio gets too far out of line. Alternatively, the split of external financing between debt and equity can be handled within the model. However, this approach may become rather complicated because share issues are only made occasionally and in most years only debt is raised. To forecast the split accurately both in terms of amount and timing may be extremely difficult and of rather little benefit.

Sophisticated reserve adjustments such as scrip issues or fixed asset revaluations are usually best left out of spreadsheet forecasting models. They rarely have any cash flow effect and can easily disrupt other relationships in the model. If, for any reason, they must be included then they should be treated as exogenous events. Consequently it is usually best to restrict reserve movements to just the increase caused by adding the retained profit for the year.

Bank overdraft is the last item to be forecast and is the easiest of all. It is simply whatever figure is necessary to make the balance sheet balance! Readers who are not very familiar with accounting and finance may find this proposal rather surprising. It may even sound like cheating. However, after a moment's thought, it can be seen to be perfectly correct.

Up to this point each figure in the balance sheet was forecast as whatever was necessary to support the level of activity shown in the profit and loss account. For example, the fixed-asset level was determined by the management's opinion of what was needed, stock was determined to suit the level of activity and so forth. No consideration was given to whether the company could afford that level of resources. However, that question now has to be faced because the consequence is that the company must borrow whatever is necessary to finance the assets which have been put on the books.

When the necessary debt level is calculated, it may of course turn out to be unrealistic. The forecast will then have to be rejected and the whole process started again to try to find an alternative solution with a more modest financing need. This may seem a very long-winded approach but the whole point of spreadsheet models is that a great many different assumptions can be tried out quite quickly. Therefore it does not take long to find a sensible forecast and in the process to discover both the management and the environment factors which matter.

Sensitivity Analysis and the Spreadsheet Model

Now that each element of the forecasting model for Watlington has been discussed it is possible to put everything together and calculate the forecasts for 1985 and 1986. This has been done in figure 8.3. The final values that would appear on the screen are shown in the left-hand panel. The formulae which generated those values are shown in the right-hand panel. Only the last two columns are shown explicitly because there are no formulae in the first three columns.

The main purpose of the model was to forecast Watlington's bank overdraft requirement in 1985 and 1986 and specifically to confirm that the limit of £150,000 would be appropriate. In fact it is clear from

	A	B	C	D	E		
1	WATLINGTON LIMITED						
2							
3	PROFIT AND LOSS ACCOUNTS	1983	1984	1985	1986	1985	1986
4	Sales	2500	2875	3306	3802	1.15*C4	1.15*D4
5	Cost of goods sold	1625	1869	2149	2471	0.65*D4	0.65*E4
6							
7	GROSS PROFIT	875	1006	1157	1331	+D4−D5	+E4−E5
8	Depreciation	206	237	303	353	0.366*D25	0.366*E25
9	Interest charge	4	7	23	49	0.12*(C34+D34)/2	0.12*(D34+E34)/2
10	Other costs	500	575	661	760	0.2*D4	0.2*E4
11							
12	NET PROFIT	165	187	170	169	+D7−D8−D9−D10	+E7−E8−E9−E10
13	Taxation	68	77	70	69	0.41*D12	0.41*E12
14							
15	EARNINGS	97	110	100	100	+D12−D13	+E12−E13
16	Dividend	50	50	50	50	50	50
17							
18	RETAINED EARNINGS	47	60	50	50	+D15−D16	+E15−E16
19							
20							
21	BALANCE SHEETS	1983	1984	1985	1985	1985	1985
22	Fixed assets at cost	1102	1267	1623	1888	+D25/0.555	+E25/0.555
23	Accumulated depreciation	490	563	722	840	+D22−D25	+E22−E25
24							
25	NET FIXED ASSETS	612	704	901	1048	+C25+500−D8	+D25+500−E8
26	Stock	312	280	412	474	70*D5/365	70*E5/365
27	Debtors	185	213	245	281	27*D4/365	27*E4/365
28	Cash	20	23	26	30	2.9*D4/365	2.9*E4/365
29							
30	TOTAL ASSETS	1129	1220	1584	1833	@ SUM (D25..D28)	@ SUM (E25..E28)
31							
32	Ordinary shares	600	600	600	600	600	600
33	Reserves	130	190	240	290	+C33+D18	+D33+E18
34	Bank overdraft	62	51	330	484	+D30−D32−D33−D35−D36−D37	+E30−E32−E33−E35−E36−E37
35	Creditors	233	268	308	354	34*D4/365	34*E4/365
36	Tax due	54	61	56	55	0.8*D13	0.8*E13
37	Dividend due	50	50	50	50	+D16	+E16
38							
39	LIABILITIES AND EQUITY	1129	1220	1584	1833	@ SUM (D32..D37)	@ SUM (E32..E37)
40							

Figure 8.3 The completed spreadsheet for Watlington.

figure 8.3 that this figure is likely to be totally inadequate. Given the assumptions, the model is forecasting an overdraft of £330,000 in 1985 and £484,000 in 1986. Thus either Watlington's management will have to alter their plans or else there is something wrong with the assumptions.

It is, of course, inevitable that at least some of the assumptions are wrong. However, the important question is whether any of them could be wrong enough to matter. In other words, are there plausible alternative assumptions that would have led to dramatically different conclusions about the overdraft level? If not, then the results are robust and the management have a real cause for concern.

In order to find out whether the forecast is robust it is necessary to try some different values in the model. One obvious possibility is to follow up the idea that stock could be held at the 1984 level of 55 days. This would require the formula in cell D26 to be altered to become 55*D5/365 and the one in E26 to be altered to 55*E5/365, but no other changes would be required. Despite the simplicity of these changes their effects are quite far-reaching. The reduced stock level directly saves a significant amount of overdraft. As a result the interest charge is lowered. This raises the profit and in turn lowers the overdraft still further. Consequently the 1986 overdraft level would be reduced by £118,000 despite the stock only being reduced by £102,000.

Apart from changing the stock levels, there are a number of other alternative assumptions which need investigating. Indeed, there are so many that even with a computer to do the calculations the task is formidable. In general the easiest approach is to take one assumption at a time, leaving everything else set at its most likely value. This allows the effect of each to be isolated from the others.

For example, the top left-hand panel of figure 8.4 shows the effect on the forecast overdraft levels of altering the stock days while holding everything else constant. In a similar way, the other panels in figure 8.4 show the effect of altering other assumptions. From them it is clear that even quite small changes are important in some cases. For example, an alteration in the cost of goods sold percentage from 65 per cent to 69 per cent would increase the forecast 1986 overdraft level to £758,000. By contrast, altering the interest rate from the most optimistic to the most pessimistic level makes relatively little difference.

The main shortcoming of this approach is that it does not allow for more than one variable to be altered at the same time. For instance, one cannot be entirely sure that the cost of goods sold percentage would still be as critical if the stock, debtors and creditor days were given different values. If the model is not too complicated this can

BANK OVERDRAFT ASSUMING DIFFERENT STOCK DAYS

STOCK DAYS		1985	1986
Most likely value	70	330	484
Very pessimistic value	90	454	638
Fairly pessimistic value	80	393	561
Fairly optimistic value	60	267	405
Very optimistic value	50	205	327

BANK OVERDRAFT ASSUMING DIFFERENT SALES GROWTH RATES

SALES GROWTH RATES		1985	1986
Most likely value	15	330	484
Very pessimistic value	5	336	528
Fairly pessimistic value	10	333	509
Fairly optimistic value	20	327	461
Very optimistic value	25	323	445

BANK OVERDRAFT ASSUMING DIFFERENT DEBTOR DAYS

DEBTOR DAYS		1985	1986
Most likely value	27	330	484
Very pessimistic value	33	387	554
Fairly pessimistic value	30	359	520
Fairly optimistic value	24	300	448
Very optimistic value	21	271	412

BANK OVERDRAFT ASSUMING DIFFERENT CGS PERCENTAGES

CGS PERCENTAGES		1985	1986
Most likely value	65	330	484
Very pessimistic value	69	484	758
Fairly pessimistic value	67	408	622
Fairly optimistic value	63	252	345
Very optimistic value	61	176	208

BANK OVERDRAFT ASSUMING DIFFERENT CREDITOR DAYS

CREDITOR DAYS		1985	1986
Most likely value	34	330	484
Very pessimistic value	27	397	567
Fairly pessimistic value	31	359	520
Fairly optimistic value	37	301	448
Very optimistic value	40	272	411

BANK OVERDRAFT ASSUMING DIFFERENT INTEREST RATES

INTEREST RATES		1985	1986
Most likely value	12	330	484
Very pessimistic value	16	337	504
Fairly pessimistic value	14	334	494
Fairly optimistic value	10	326	473
Very optimistic value	8	323	462

Figure 8.4 Summary of sensitivity analysis results.

sometimes be established theoretically but this may not be easy in a spreadsheet model. In very complex models, it may not even be theoretically possible. Thus in practice, it is usually necessary to repeat the exercise illustrated in figure 8.4 for a number of different scenarios. So long as the model has been properly set up this will not be as large a task as it may seem.

In general there are three considerations which determine whether a spreadsheet model is well suited to large-scale sensitivity analysis.

1 Altering the assumptions should be as easy and error-free as possible.
2 The model should provide good feedback to show the relevant details and give warning of anything that does not make sense.
3 It should take advantage of the full power of the spreadsheet program being used so that the solution will be as fast and efficient as possible.

The model used so far does not score very well on any of these criteria.

Altering assumptions in the model in figure 8.3 is more difficult than it needs to be because every change requires the relevant formulae to be directly modified. This is both awkward and error-prone. There is also no easy way of telling from the model's printout which assumptions have been used in each particular case. Both these shortcoming could easily be cured by using a separate part of the spreadsheet for a table of assumptions and then rewriting the formulae so that they relate to that table. For example, suppose that the assumed figure for stock days in 1985 was shown in the table as, say, D50. The formula in D6 (figure 8.3) could be rewritten as +D50*D5/365. Consequently, changing D50 would both display the current assumption and appropriately alter the current value of stock.

If the assumptions to be altered are removed into a separate part of the spreadsheet a further benefit arises. The model itself can be 'protected' so that no-one can inadvertently make any changes to the formulae. Thus the risk of accidents is much reduced.

The second criterion for a good model is the provision of good feedback. This means that it must be easy to identify interesting or important results as well as entry errors or any evidence that the model is not working correctly. Often the most effective method is to design the model so that the input assumptions and a summary of key output variables are displayed alongside each other on a single screen. This allows changes to be made and the consequences to be seen immediately alongside those changes.

Graphs also offer a powerful way of having a quick look at several figures. They often show up implausible or interesting trends more easily than the numbers themselves. In a similar way some well-chosen ratios, or other derived information, may offer additional insights and help to highlight implausible results. However, the critical factor is that the output information must not only be useful, it must be quick to display and easy to absorb. Otherwise the result of analysing a few dozen options may not be a deep understanding but a more thorough confusion!

The final consideration is to ensure that effective use is made of the considerable power of spreadsheet packages. In some spreadsheet applications efficiency may not be too important. However, in sensitivity analysis the model is likely to be modified and recalculated so many times that quite small improvements can accumulate to give worthwhile time savings. The most obvious place to look for such savings is in the recalculation process. In Lotus 1–2–3 this is optimized by the program so there is no particular speed advantage in laying out the model in one way rather than another.

Less sophisticated spreadsheet programs are likely to recalculate the sheet, either row by row, or column by column. When this happens the speed with which the model converges to a solution can be significantly improved by rearranging the formulae. The trick is to ensure that, wherever possible, the formulae do not make forward references to other cells which have not, at that time, been evaluated. This may be in conflict with the more important criterion of making the model easy to understand so a sensible balance has to be struck.

Some spreadsheet programs have special features which can remove much of the tedium from sensitivity analysis. A good example is the 'Data Table' feature of Lotus 1–2–3. This allows a table to be created which automatically shows the values of certain variables under different assumptions. It is possible to tabulate several variables while allowing one assumption to vary, or to tabulate one variable which allows two assumptions to vary. The first of these was used to create the tables in figure 8.4 which are presented almost exactly as they were produced by a microcomputer.

In addition to the data table feature, Lotus 1–2–3 has other features which can make sensitivity analysis much more effective. One of these is to pre-set a series of graphs so that each can be viewed at the touch of a single key. This allows some or all of the graphs for any forecast to be viewed extremely easily.

Another useful feature is the ability to create what are known as

'Keyboard macros', which are essentially just pre-defined strings of instructions. These are helpful because the instruction sequences used in sensitivity analysis are usually fairly repetitive. Consequently, it is often possible to devise appropriate keyboard macros which allow quite complicated action to be carried out with a single key stroke.

Conclusion

There is no doubt that microcomputer spreadsheet programs can help enormously in the task of managing business forecasts. This is not because they improve the accuracy of forecasts. They do not. It is because they allow managers to work through the implications of alternative outcomes and to discover which assumptions matter and which do not.

Large-scale corporate models offer the same opportunities and allow much more sophisticated models of the business to be used. However, sometimes their very complexity is a disadvantage. A spreadsheet model of the type described in this chapter can easily be created and used by the manager; it requires no assistance from the computer department.

For this reason such a model will usually be better understood than a large-scale model and it may also be easier for the manager to modify. Hence it may be useful to think of spreadsheet models as somewhat like the proverbial back of an envelope calculation. They may be a bit crude by big computer standards but their solutions are quickly available and relevant.

Notes

1 The proof of this statement requires no more than simple algebra:

total cost (t) = fixed cost (t) + variable unit cost (t)* sales volume (t)

and

sales value (t) = sales price (t)* sales volume (t)

Hence:

$$\text{total cost } (t) = \text{fixed cost } (t) + \text{variable unit cost } (t)* \frac{\text{sales value } (t)}{\text{sales price } (t)}$$

If the cost curve of two different dates (t_1 and t_2 are to have the same slope it follows that the necessary condition is:

$$\frac{\text{variable unit cost } (t_1)}{\text{variable unit cost } (t_2)} = \frac{\text{sales price } (t_1)}{\text{sales price } (t_2)}$$

2 It is interesting to note that as expected the spurious relationship between actual costs and sales indicates a lower fixed cost, a higher variable unit cost and a higher R squared than the inflation-adjusted figure. The regression equation is

$$\text{cost} = 597 + 0.4999 * \text{sales} \qquad \text{with } R \text{ squared} = 0.99$$

3 Constant investment in each year would be a special case of this assumption where the growth rate is zero per cent so that investment each year is constant.

CHAPTER 9

Forecasting the Total UK Sales of an Alcoholic Beverage

This case study is based upon a project which took place recently in the UK. The project was sponsored by one of the main producers of a certain alcoholic beverage. The organization is diversified and has many other products. The results of the project were for the exclusive use of the organization and consequently the project has had to be slightly disguised to preserve confidentiality.

The terms of reference were to forecast the industry-wide UK sales volumes for this particular well-established alcoholic beverage. The forecasts produced were to be used as the basis for short- to medium-term production and marketing decisions.

The beverage takes a relatively short time (a matter of weeks) to produce and distribute. Stock levels are kept low partly because the product can deteriorate, albeit slowly, and partly because the costs of holding stocks are high compared to production costs. The need for low stock levels together with fierce competition from other producers has meant that it is imperative to respond quickly, in terms of both production and marketing, to changes in demand. This was the primary reason for the forecasting project being set in motion.

The beverage is not a new one and a substantial amount of data was available. In particular, industry sales volumes (quarterly) going back several years could be obtained easily. Furthermore, most people in the industry believed the data to be accurate and reliable. Data for the last 15 years are shown in table 9.1. They are in unspecified units and have been rounded for ease of manipulation. This data record was not all that was available. The project team had access to all the organization's data concerning the product as well as other generally available data about the industry and the economic climate.

The approach to this forecasting was to use the nine-point checklist of chapter 1. In going through these steps other techniques and ideas

Table 9.1   Sales volume (unspecified units)

Year	Quarter 1	2	3	4	Total
1970	9	10	12	11	42
1971	12	15	16	13	56
1972	16	17	20	16	69
1973	18	21	22	17	78
1974	21	23	27	22	93
1975	25	27	32	26	110
1976	26	29	35	27	117
1977	28	35	40	29	132
1978	33	41	45	33	152
1979	32	42	53	38	165
1980	33	42	54	40	169
1981	32	45	58	41	176
1982	34	46	57	44	181
1983	36	48	61	45	190
1984	37	49	63	48	197

described in previous chapters will be used. Forecasting techniques can rarely be applied in strict textbook fashion. From time to time they have had to be adapted to reflect this particular situation.

1 Analyse the Decision-taking System

The purpose of this analysis was to ensure that the forecasts really did serve the decision process as intended, and were not unconnected and peripheral. Important side benefits often accrue from such analyses. Inconsistencies in the way decisions are taken and in the organizational structure may come to light. A whole forecasting project may have to be postponed pending the resolution of these wider issues. The description of this case continues on the assumption that such matters have been resolved.

A thorough analysis of a decision-taking system involves systems theory. A lower level approach of listing the decisions directly and indirectly affected by the forecasts is described here. The list was determined from an exhaustive study of the organizational structure and the job descriptions associated with relevant parts of it. The analysis of the decision-taking process was discussed and checked carefully with those involved. It formed the input information for step 2, determining the forecasts required.

2 Determine the Forecasts Required

The decisions all had a time horizon of at most one year. The forecasts had therefore to be for one year ahead.

The production decisions required monthly forecasts, the distribution and marketing decisions quarterly forecasts. This suggested that the system should produce monthly forecasts, aggregating in the case of the latter. The timing of the decisions within the month or quarter dictated the time at which the forecasts were to reach the decision-takers.

At this stage the question may arise of exactly which variable to forecast. For example, consumption of a product can mean the amount leaving the factory, or the amount received by wholesalers, or the amount received by the retailer, or the amount consumed by the final user. The last may seem to be the best but it is difficult to measure. The situation is further confused when the producer may own some wholesale or retail outlets. In this case the forecast variable was taken to be the quantity of the product entering retail outlets.

3 Conceptualize

At this stage consideration was given to the factors which influenced the forecast variable; no thought was given to data availability. An ideal situation was being envisaged. A list of factors was drawn up after extensive discussion, even brainstorming sessions, with industry experts. The discussions included consideration of similar forecasting projects in the organization, in the industry and elsewhere.

An alcoholic beverage is not strictly essential to the maintenance of life. It is a luxury product. As such its consumption will be affected by economic circumstances. It would be strange if advertising and promotions did not result in changes in demand. In addition the variability of the production, advertising and promotions of the different competitors must have an effect. In particular the launch of a new product changes the state of the market. It is not just competing producers of the beverage which are important: competition in the form of other products must also have an influence.

Table 9.2   The decision-taking system

Main decisions	Related decisions
1 Production levels for 1 year ahead. (monthly)	Materials requirements Manpower requirements Pre-production operating activities Machinery maintenance Warehousing requirements Short-term financial planning
2 Distribution quantities (quarterly)	Warehousing requirements Transport needs Short-term financial planning
3 Marketing action (quarterly)	Advertising Promotions

The data record in table 9.1 makes it clear that there is a seasonal effect. In other words the time of year and perhaps the weather are relevant factors. Special events may have had a temporary influence: a change in excise duty as a result of a national budget is an obvious example. More tentatively, national success in sporting tournaments is rumoured to have an effect on the consumption of alcoholic beverages.

There was also a case for taking a purely time series approach to the forecast. First, the seasonal effect would be handled easily by such methods. Second, the time horizon for the forecasts was short – less than one year. Within such a period there was little time for other variables to bring their influence to bear. To some extent, therefore, sales volume would have a momentum of its own. In other words 'habit' would be a major influence on buying behaviour in the short term. Third, a time series approach would give a forecast on the basis of the future being like the past. Such a forecast would be the starting point for judging the effect of changing circumstances.

4 Ascertain Data Availability

The ideals which were the subject of step 3 were to be restricted by the availability (or lack of availability) of data. The search for data records relating to the factors of step 3 revealed what the restrictions were.

Industry data on advertising and promotions were not available. The organization's own data on advertising and promotions had been aggregated and could not be separated. Individually, data from competitors were available for some factors (production levels, new products), but not for others (advertising, promotions). Where competitive data were available, however, they were not at hand sufficiently early to be used. They did not become available within the one-year time horizon of the forecasts.

The data which were both available and usable were the organization's own aggregated data on advertising and promotions and nationally available data on the economic climate. In the case of the former only quarterly data could be obtained. Unfortunately, monthly forecasts were wanted. Regretfully it had to be decided to produce only quarterly forecasts.

Consideration of table 9.1 suggested that some of the earlier data should not be used for the forecasts. This was because the data appear to behave differently before and after the mid-1970s. This view is reinforced by figure 9.1, the graph of table 9.1. First, the increase in sales volume in the early 1970s was higher than subsequently. The average annual increase between 1970 and 1975 was 14; the average annual increase between 1979 and 1984 was six. Second, the seasonal pattern appears more marked in the post-1975 period. Whatever the reasons for this change, there was no point in requiring the forecasting techniques to account for it if the earlier behaviour no longer applied. Some early data could therefore be excluded. Exactly which data to exclude was not an easy question to answer. The change in growth seemed to take place around 1978; the change in seasonality seemed to take place around 1976. Because of the constant need to have as much data as possible and because of the importance of seasonality in making forecasts one year ahead in this context, the decision was taken to exclude data from 1975 and earlier.

5 Decide Which Technique to Use

There were good reasons for employing both a time series and a causal modelling approach to the problem. It was agreed to use both and then judge which appeared the more accurate.

A time series technique would have to have a number of characteristics. It would have to handle the trend evident from table 9.1. It would also have to deal with the seasonal effect. There may or may not be a cycle in the data. However, the decision to restrict the data

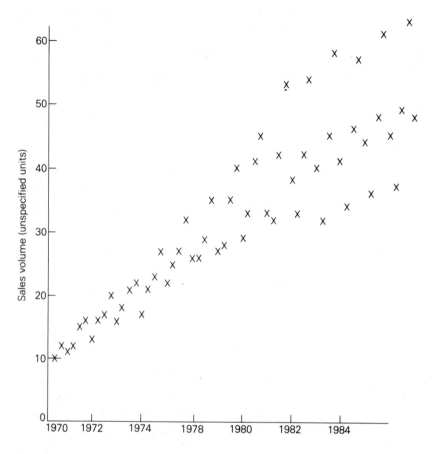

Figure 9.1   Quarterly sales (see table 9.1).

record to the period 1976–84 meant that it would be difficult to determine any cyclical effect (these effects are often five or seven years in length). What was required was a technique which could handle trend and seasonality but not cycles. The obvious choice was the Holt–Winters technique.

The causal modelling technique was multiple regression analysis with two independent variables. The first independent variable was the gross domestic product (GDP) of the UK, as a measure of the economic climate. Other economic variables can be used in this role but GDP is the most usual. The second independent variable was the sum of advertising and promotional expenditures (ADV/PRO) of the organization. Scatter diagrams relating the dependent variable with each independent variable in turn verified that it was reasonable to consider GDP and ADV/PRO as independent variables. In spite of this it should be noted that industry sales were to be forecast, but the organization's data on advertising and promotions were being used.

Other potential independent variables had to be ignored because the relevant data were not available.

6 Test the Accuracy

Because two approaches (time series and causal modelling) were being employed, there were two stages in testing the accuracy of the forecasts. First, it had to be determined which Holt–Winters model (i.e. what values for the smoothing constants) was the best and whether one or both of the independent variables should be included in the regression model. Second, the best Holt–Winters model had to be compared with the best regression model.

Which Holt–Winters Model?

The Holt–Winters model works with three smoothing constants, one each for the main series, the trend and the seasonality. To decide on the values for the constants some experimentation was needed. Several different sets of values were tried and the forecasting accuracy of each compared. The accuracy was measured via the mean square (MSE) or the mean absolute deviation (MAD) of the one step ahead forecast errors.

This process was described in chapter 6 but a brief reminder is given here. For any set of parameters, go through the data record time period by time period and at each calculate a forecast for one period ahead. Find the forecast error by subtracting the forecast from the actual. Measure the scatter of these errors for the whole series by calculating the mean square error (the average squared error) or the mean absolute deviation (the average of the absolute values of the errors). Repeat with other parameter sets. Choose the set for which one or both of these statistics is the lowest.

It is best to try a wide range of parameter sets and settle on the one that seems the best. Table 9.3 shows the results of this process for the data of table 9.1. The table shows the parameter sets in three groups. For the first group the smoothing constant for the main series was varied; for the second, that for the trend was varied keeping the series

Table 9.3   Determining the accuracy of the Holt–Winters model

Smoothing constants			MAD	MSE
0.5	0.2	0.2	6	51
0.4	0.2	0.2	5	42
0.3	0.2	0.2	5	35
0.2	0.2	0.2	4	33
0.1	0.2	0.2	5	46
0.2	0.4	0.2	4	30
0.2	0.3	0.2	4	31
0.2	0.1	0.2	5	40
0.2	0.5	0.2	4	30
0.2	0.6	0.2	4	30
0.2	0.4	0.5	3	15*
0.2	0.4	0.4	3	17
0.2	0.4	0.3	4	22
0.2	0.4	0.1	6	46

* Best parameter set

constant at its 'best' level; finally the constant for seasonality was varied keeping the other two at their 'best' level. The parameter set with the lowest MAD and MSE was (0.2, 0.4, 0.5). The Holt–Winters model with these parameters would appear to be the best. Note that the procedure for finding these parameter values is an approximate one. There is no guarantee that the truly optimum set has been found. To ensure that this had been done would have required an exhaustive comparison of all possible parameter sets.

Which Regression Model?

There are three possible regression models:

1 GDP as independent variable.

2 ADV/PRO as independent variable.

3 GDP and ADV/PRO as independent variables.

They should be compared using the following basic criteria:

Plausibility of models.

Closeness of fit – using R squared.

Randomness of residuals – by inspection.

t values greater than 2.0.

Table 9.4 shows how the three models compare according to these criteria. The first model, using GDP as the only independent variable, is inadequate. The fit is not a close one (R squared = 0.27). Nor are the residuals random. They exhibit a seasonal pattern in that the residuals for quarter 1 are all negative, for quarter 3 all positive.

The second model, using ADV/PRO as the independent variable, is good. The fit is a close one and the residuals are random.

The third model, with GDP and ADV/PRO as independent variables, is slightly better than the second, having a marginally higher R^2.

In all models the t values are greater than 2, indicating that it was right to include the independent variables.

Finally, since these are regression models, they should be checked for any of the reservations – lack of causality, spuriousness etc. described in chapter 3. There may indeed be a problem with causality. The second and third models are superior because the ADV/PRO variable captures the seasonality which was a problem in the first. It is not clear whether it is the seasonality or the expenditure on advertising and promotion which explains the changes in sales volumes. There will be no difficulty if advertising and promotion expenditures continue to be determined with seasonal variations as in the past, but if the method of allocation changes then both models will be inadequate. A new model, dealing with advertising/promotion and seasonality separately, would have to be tested.

Meanwhile the model with two independent variables seemed to be the best. The results of this regression analysis are shown in more detail in table 9.5.

Table 9.4   Regression models

Criterion	Model (independent variable(s))		
	GDP	ADV/PRO	GDP, ADV/PRO
Plausibility	Yes	Yes	Yes
R squared	0.27	0.91	0.93
Random residuals	No (seasonality)	Yes	Yes
t values	Yes	Yes	Yes

Table 9.5   Output of the regression model linking sales to GDP and ADV/PRO

Sales volume = $-47.4 + 0.53 \times$ GDP + $17.3 \times$ ADV/PRO
$\qquad\qquad\qquad\qquad (t = 3.2) \qquad\quad (t = 17.7)$

R squared   = 0.93

Residuals:

Year	Quarter			
	1	2	3	4
1976	-0.3	-4.2	-0.4	-0.6
1977	2.4	-1.3	1.7	-4.6
1978	2.6	4.3	-0.5	1.4
1979	-1.1	-5.3	4.7	1.7
1980	-2.9	1.8	0.7	2.7
1981	-1.9	2.8	1.3	3.0
1982	-2.6	-1.2	-0.7	-0.3
1983	1.4	-2.2	0	-0.1
1984	-1.4	-5.0	3.5	0.8

Best Overall? Time Series or Regression?

The best time series model was the Holt–Winters model with smoothing constants 0.2 (for the series), 0.4 (for the trend) and 0.5 (for the seasonality); the best regression model related sales volume to GDP and total expenditure on advertising and promotion. To choose between these two, an independent test of accuracy was used. This meant that the latest data (1984) were kept apart and the data up to then (1976–83) used as the basis for forecasting 1984. The better model was the one that provided forecasts for 1984 which were closer to the actual sales volumes. There were two reasons for comparing the models in this way.

1 The test is independent in the sense that the data being forecast (1984) are not used in establishing the forecasting model. Contrast this with the use of R squared. All of the data, 1976–84, are used to calculate the coefficients of the model; the residuals are then calculated and R squared measures how close this model is to the same 1976–84 data. This is not an independent measure of accuracy.
2 The accuracy of smoothing techniques is usually measured through the mean square error or mean absolute deviation; the accuracy of regression models is measured by R squared. These two types of

measures are not directly comparable. On the other hand the independent test of accuracy does provide a directly comparable measure – closeness to the 1984 data.

The details of the test are as follows. The 1976–83 data were used for each of the two models as the basis of a forecast for each of the four quarters of 1984. The closeness of the two sets of forecasts to the actual 1984 data was measured using the mean square error and the mean absolute deviation. The model for which both these measures were smaller was chosen as the better to use in practice. Should the two measures have contradicted one another then this would have meant that the model with the lower MSE tended to be closer to extreme values whereas the model with the lower MAD tended to be closer on average to all values.

Table 9.6   Comparing time series and regression models

Quarter	Actual	Time series			Regression		
(of 1984)		F'cast	Error	Error²	F'cast	Error	Error²
1	37	38	−1	1	39	−2	4
2	49	50	−1	1	54	−5	25
3	63	63	0	0	60	3	9
4	48	47	1	1	47	1	1
	MAD = 3/4	MSE = 3/4		MAD = 11/4		MSE = 39/4	
	= 0.75	= 0.75		= 2.75		= 9.75	

Table 9.6 shows the results of this test. The Holt–Winters time series was clearly superior to the regression model. Both measures, MAD and MSE, demonstrated that it gave the best forecasts for the already known 1984 data. The Holt–Winters technique, with smoothing constants 0.2, 0.4, 0.5, was chosen to make forecasts for 1985. The whole of the data series, including, of course, 1984, was used in doing this. These forecasts are shown in table 9.7.

Table 9.7   1985 forecasts

Quarter (of 1985)	Forecast
1	39
2	52
3	66
4	49

7 Incorporate Judgements into the Forecast

To incorporate judgements into a forecast, there are two basic tasks. The first is to draw all the judgements together and try to form a consensus. This can be done through one of the qualitative forecasting techniques. The second task is to make an adjustment, if necessary, to the forecast. This can be accomplished by getting those affected by the forecast to agree to the change and then, most important of all, to make them accountable for the change. It is vital that the accuracy of the alterations be monitored.

The situation in this case was somewhat different from that of a purely internal forecast. Here it was not the organization's own sales which were being predicted but industry sales. The body of experts whose views had to be considered went well beyond people inside the organization. Assembling the judgements, obtaining a consensus, making people accountable for their views was a difficult, if not impossible, task. Nevertheless, the approach was as outlined above. First, the judgements were brought together; second, decisions to adjust the statistically derived forecasts were made.

Table 9.8 summarizes some of the judgements made about the future of this industry. Sometimes the judgements were expressed in words rather than in convenient percentage growth terms. When this happened a quantitative forecast had to be derived from the words. Table 9.8 shows the source of each judgement, the verbal forecast where one existed and a forecast in terms of percentage growth whether actual or derived. Because some of the percentage growth figures had to be distilled from verbally expressed views, there was some doubt about some of the percentages. For example, does 'No cause for optimism' translate into zero per cent growth?

To obtain a consensus from these data, a modified version of Delphi was used. All the experts represented in the table were approached, presented with the views of the others and asked if they wished to adjust their opinions. As a result some of the more extreme views were altered. However, no true consensus was achieved. The average growth forecast was 3 per cent with a variation from zero to 4 per cent.

The second stage, the adjustment of the statistical forecasts, was carried out by people within the organization. They were to be accountable for any changes made; it was not, of course, possible to make the external experts accountable for their views within the context of the organization.

As it was, these judgements did not result in any adjustments being made to the first Holt–Winters forecasts produced. While the Holt–Winters forecasts showed no more than a 1 per cent increase over 1984, the increase was from an unusually high base. Over three years the forecast is equivalent to a 3 per cent per annum growth rate. For this reason in particular the statistical forecast was left alone. The seasonal element in the forecast would, in any case, have had to be left entirely to the statistical technique.

Table 9.8   Experts' opinions of industry prospects

Source	Verbal forecast	% growth p.a.
Business pages of newspapers		
1	Slight decline in volume next year	−1 to −2
2	Stagnation for two to three years	0
3	Continuing as in recent years	4
4	No significant changes in the situation	4
Business journals:		
1	No cause for optimism	0 (?)
2	No improvement in prospects	3
Industry experts:		
1	Specific forecast	4
2	Specific forecast	5
3	Specific forecast	5
Stockbrokers:		
1	Unlikely to sustain even recent modest growth	1
2	Unchanged situation	4

Had adjustments been made, the people in the organization who made them would have had to give account of themselves if their judgement proved incorrect (and accepted the plaudits had their judgement proved correct).

8 Implement the Forecast

Chapter 7 suggested that there were four questions to be asked and answered in implementing a forecast.

What are the problems?

Do all the participants agree on the problems?

What are the possible solutions to the problems?

Can a consensus on an action plan be obtained?

Implementation in this case began with the drawing up of a list of everyone affected by the forecasts. Nearly all the main functional departments: finance, marketing, production, corporate planning, were represented on the list. Those on the list were then interviewed. The purpose was solely to find out what difficulties they thought might block the successful working of the system. The style of interviewing was neutral. No attempt was made to lead the interviewees, nor to sell the forecasting system to them, nor to encourage them to say nice things about it. Such approaches would have resulted in their putting up defensive barriers and not revealing their real views.

As could have been easily predicted, there were many problems; but only the two main types will be described. First, there was disagreement about the effect of a series of new brands that were about to be introduced both by the organization itself and by competitors. Second, there were internal political problems. The organizational structure had recently been changed. Some suspicion and some sparring were evident.

The most usual problem, lack of belief in new techniques and technology on the part of the users, was absent in this case. Previous successful forecasting meant that managers were prepared to give it a try, even to welcome it. As a result there was almost no tension between producers and users. Perhaps this was also because the uncertainty over the organizational structure tended to dwarf other issues. Agreement on what the problems were was quickly reached. The search for solutions, however, presented greater difficulties. It was not a question of deciding between different solutions but of finding them in the first place.

Finally, the problem of the new brands was solved by creating two sets of forecast, each relating to a different set of assumptions about the effect of the new brands. In effect the solution was a form of the technique of scenario writing. Contingency plans were to be prepared so that the organization could respond to either scenario. The problem of the political difficulties went far beyond the forecasting project. It was something that, at that time, had its affect on all the organization's activities. Involving the users from the start minimized the effect of these problems since the participants felt more like a team than they would otherwise have done. There was little more that could be done. Undoubtedly this particular issue did, in some small way, cast its shadow over the project and reduce the effectiveness of the forecasting.

9 Monitor Performance

Monitoring is probably the most tedious stage of the nine, being based on soliciting and recording a considerable amount of information. Thoroughness and persistence are the virtues required. The performance of this forecasting system was monitored through three separate reports.

1 An annual report showed the accuracy of the forecasts as measured by the mean absolute deviation (MAD). The MAD achieved was compared with the MAD that had been expected given the measurement of accuracy described in stage 6. As well as this indication of the average accuracy, exceptional inaccuracies were reported with suggested reasons for their occurrence. If some particular reason had appeared consistently, the intention was to adjust the forecasting system accordingly. For example, had there been changes in the trend to which the system had responded too slowly, then the smoothing constant for the trend equation would have been increased. The point is that, although the smoothing constant as set had been fine for the historical data, it might no longer be right if the trend started to behave in a slightly different way. An adjustment to it would then have to be considered. If the trend started to behave in a radically different way the whole basis of the system (the use of Holt–Winters) would have to be re-evaluated.

2 An annual report showed the performance of the judges, those who had proposed qualitative adjustments to the forecasts. This meant that their judgemental forecasts had to be recorded from minutes of meetings and compared with what had happened. Over time the identity of the good judgemental forecasters began to emerge. Their views then carried greater weight in later forecasts. Many of them outperformed the statistical forecasts. However, before scrapping the statistical system it had to be borne in mind that these judgements were being made as an amendment to the Holt–Winters output. It is one thing to be able to make marginal improvements to

an existing forecast; it is quite another to beat the existing forecast when working in isolation from it.

3 After the system had been in operation for a year a survey of users was carried out by an independent party. The users were asked for their perceptions of the system. Exactly how did they use the forecasts? What were the strengths and weaknesses of the system? How could it be improved? Did they think it had been successful in achieving its objectives? and so on. This demonstrated that the system did have credibility amongst the users and did support their decisions. Such a survey was to be repeated in the future when it was felt that the whole system was due for review and re-appraisal.

Conclusion

The system has now been in operation for some time and is perceived to have been successful. On the whole the forecasts have been accurate. The incorporation of judgements has been especially useful in making allowance for exceptional circumstances such as strikes and extraordinary national budgets.

It should be emphasized that it is only for short-term forecasts that a time series method would have worked out so well. For medium-term forecasts beyond a year ahead a causal model would have undoubtedly been better. Even for a short-term forecast, however, recent uncertainty and volatility in the UK economic environment eventually caused problems and adjustments had to be made to the Holt–Winters model. For important medium-term forecasts on which the expenditure of a great deal of money is justified it may be worthwhile to use all three approaches to forecasting: causal, time series and qualitative. If all give similar output, there is mutual confirmation of the correct forecast; if they give different outputs then the process of reconciling them will be a valuable way for the managers involved to gain a better understanding of the future.

This description has covered the important aspects of the case, but not all the aspects. The details left out have not been omitted because of lack of space, but because they are of concern to statisticians rather than managers. For example, statistical tests of randomness have been excluded. It was perfectly possible to determine randomness and non-randomness visually; statistical confirmation would have been a bonus but it was not a necessity. Another omission was that techniques other than Holt–Winters and some causal modelling were considered, but since they were found to be inferior the detail of the comparisons has not been shown. For example, decomposition was found to be less accurate than Holt–Winters. The items included are, however, all the things of which a manager would need to be aware in order to be able to engage in sensible discussions with forecasting experts. If managers concentrate on managerial issues while at the same time having just sufficient technical knowledge to be able to relate to forecasting experts, their potential contribution to forecasting projects is enormous.

CHAPTER 10

Data Sources for Forecasting

In many forecasting studies, collecting the necessary input data can represent a far greater task than deciding which forecasting technique to use. Obviously the data needs will vary a great deal from case to case but usually there are a considerable number of potentially useful sources available. Furthermore, the provision of information, particularly via on-line computer databases, is now big business and in recent years there has been a steady stream of new sources.

It would be impossible to give details of every source that might be useful for any forecast. However, in this chapter an attempt has been made to provide a reasonable number of starting points in the search for data. About 100 useful sources are listed along with their addresses, telephone numbers and, where appropriate, telex numbers. A brief description of each source is also given. Most of the sources listed are prepared to give further details and advice by telephone and many of them will provide brochures and other information by post.

Addresses, telephone numbers and the sources themselves change over time so an important first step in any study is to check the current availability of the sources. A number of libraries and directories are included in this list and these will usually allow the availability to be checked quite easily. Once a source is confirmed as still existing it is well worth spending a little time on the telephone asking for the latest particulars, because some of the information is quite expensive and needs to be carefully chosen.

Perhaps the most obvious place to begin a search for data is in a good business library. There are several in the UK that have excellent collections of business data and some which contain only specialized data. In addition, there are an increasing number of information consultants, often attached to libraries, who for a suitable fee will carry out data searches. Hence the first list of sources in the chapter includes a representative list of libraries and other information services. Also included in the list are a few directories which provide further information.

One type of data which is very well provided in the UK relates to individual companies – financial results, share prices and so on. Several services offer printed and computer-readable data although there are significant variations in the exact details of what each offers and the number of companies it covers. In addition to individual company data, a number of services provide financial data at an industry level. Usually this is calculated by aggregating individual company results, so in several cases both types of data are supplied by the same organization. The second and third lists in this chapter cover data for individual companies and data for aggregations of individual companies.

The next main source of information for forecasting is market research. Here the primary problem is finding the appropriate studies, because relevant work is carried out by an enormous variety of different organizations throughout the world. To deal with this a number of directories and indexes exist which help keep track of market research studies and a selection of the main ones is given in the fourth list. Some of the chief sources of market surveys and forecasts are included in the fifth list.

As well as companies, industries and markets a great deal of data is published about the country as a whole and of course similar data is available for many other countries. In the UK the majority of this information is collected by various government departments and published by Her Majesty's Stationery Office (HMSO). There is an enormous amount published and a number of excellent guides exist to explain what is available. Details of these and some of the more important sources are included in list 6.

The final list in the chapter is of sources of macroeconomic forecasts. There are several of these available which regularly make forecasts for the UK and other economies. Some have been forecasting for ten years or more and have an impressive track record, typically forecasting GDP to within 1 or 2 per cent. They vary in exactly what they forecast and how far ahead they look, so it is worth finding out which is the most appropriate; this is particularly important because, like the other sources mentioned, there is a considerable price variation between them.

List 1: Libraries, Information Services and Directories

The A–Z of UK Marketing Data
Euromonitor Publications Limited, 87–8 Turnmill Street, London EC1M 5QU. Telephone: 01-251 8024. This is one of Euromonitor's pocketbook series for handy reference data on all aspects of the UK consumer market.

The A–Z of UK Brand Leaders
Euromonitor Publications Limited, 87–8 Turnmill Street, London EC1M 5QU. Telephone: 01-251 8024. This is another Euromonitor pocketbook directory containing reference data on the UK consumer market.

Bibliographic Sources for Non-HMSO Official Publications
The British Library, Reference Division, Official Publications Library, Great Russell Street, London WC1B 3DG. Telephone: 01-636 1544 ext. 234/235. The Official Publications Library maintains a bibliography of UK government publications which are not published by HMSO. It can provide a list of non-HMSO official publications on request and will be able to help with any enquiries relating to these publications.

The British Library, Science Reference Library (Holborn)
25 Southampton Buildings, Chancery Lane, London WC2A 1AW. Telephone: 01-405 8721; Telex: 266959. The Science Reference Library has a collection of at least 25,000 periodicals, including the most extensive collection of trade journals freely available in the UK. In addition, there are trade catalogues and other literature for some 2,500 companies. The library is open to the general public, will accept telephone, telex, letter and personal enquiries and will send photocopies by post. The library produces helpful 'Aids to Readers' leaflets on various topics.

British Statistics Office
Government Buildings, Cardiff Road, Newport, Gwent NPT 1XG. Telephone: (0633) 5611 ext. 2973; Telex: 497121. This is the major official enquiry point for statistical information about industry and commerce in the UK. There are books on statistical methodology, computers and data processing; some UK company information and trade directories as well as a complete collection of *Business Monitor* periodicals. The library is open to the public and there is a telephone,

telex and letter service to answer queries. Only photocopies of official publications are available.

City Business Library
Gillett House, 55 Basinghall Street, London EC2V 5BX. Telephone: 01-638 8215 or 8216; Telex: 887955 CBLLDN. City Business Library has a comprehensive collection of directories published in the UK and subscribes to most of the services mentioned in this chapter. It is open to the general public during normal working hours and will handle telephone, telex or personal enquiries.

DIALOG Information Services
PO Box 8, Abingdon, Oxford OX13 6EG. Telephone: (0865) 730969. DIALOG is an American on-line information service with over 200 separate databases, many of which relate to industry and commerce. DIALOG has British subscribers and the main computer in California can be accessed from the UK. Ask for information on DIALOG and the more restricted service called The Knowledge Index.

Financial Times Business Information Service
Financial Times, Business Information Service, Bracken House, 10 Cannon Street, London EC4P 4BY. Telephone: 01-248 8000; Telex: 8811506. The FT service provides press cuttings, annual reports, brokers' circulars and press releases relating to companies. It can answer questions on marketing, related subjects concerning industries and markets. Financial and economic statistics such as exchange rates, money market movements and stock and share information are readily available. The FT also holds press cuttings on a large number of prominent people in industry, politics and business.

Financial Times Business Information Service Library
Bracken House, 10 Cannon Street, London EC4P 4BY. Telephone: 01-248 8000; Telex: 8811506. This is the library which supports the FT Business Information Service. It contains company files, country files, personality files, microfilm copies of the FT, Index to the FT, statistical publications, trade professional and business directories, computer terminals for accessing the major international databases. Access is by subscription.

Geisco Limited
25–9 High Street, Kingston upon Thames, Surrey KT1 1LN. Telephone: 01-546 1077. This is a worldwide computer information

service. Databases include US economic forecasts; Citibase, which contains over 4,500 historical, economic and financial time series on the US economy; Business International Corporation database which compares business performance from companies in 131 countries and has economic forecasts for 15 countries; the Currency Exchange database with currency information and related economic data and the Value Line Database-II with annual and quarterly financial histories and projections on over 1,600 major companies and financial institutions.

Holborn Reference Library
32–8 Theobald's Road, London WC1X 8PA. Telephone: 01-405 2706. A public library which contains many of the surveys and services listed in this chapter.

Libraries in the United Kingdom & The Republic of Ireland
The Library Association, 7 Ridgmount Street, London WC1E 7AE. This annual guide is readily available in most reference libraries. It gives the name, address, telephone number and name of the librarian for all public libraries in the UK and Republic of Ireland. In addition it lists University and polytechnic libraries as well as selected national, government and special libraries.

London Business School Library
Sussex Place, Regent's Park, London NW1 4SA. Telephone: 01-724 2300; Telex: 27461. This library has a large selection of books, pamphlets, periodicals and company reports. Most of the services mentioned in this chapter are available including access to various databases. It also runs the LBS Information Service which provides a comprehensive range of research and library facilities to business and commercial organizations.

London Researchers
Alan Armstrong & Associates Limited, 72–6 Park Road, London NW1 4SH. Telephone: 01-723 8530; Telex: 297635 AAALTD. London Researchers provide a comprehensive information service to business and commercial organizations. They are attached to the Business Bookshop which has an excellent stock of business books.

Manchester Business School Library
Booth Street West, Manchester M15 6PB. Telephone: 061-273 8228

ext. 264. This library subscribes to many of the services mentioned in this chapter. Contact the librarian for details of the enquiry service.

Mintel Information Services
7 Arundel Street, London WC2R 3DR. Telephone: 01-836 1814; Telex: 21405 KAEMIN G. Mintel offer a range of books on consumer marketing. This includes microfiche copies of journals, newspapers and other information as well as government publications and trade directories. Payment by subscription allows unlimited access to the library but it is also possible to make *ad hoc* enquiries. Mintel Information Services produce trade and national press digests by product area as well as a *Daily Digest* which monitors marketing activity and news.

Pergamon Infoline
Marketing Department, 1 Vandy Street, London EC2A 2DE. Telephone: 01-377 4650. This is an international on-line service operating mainly in Britain and the USA. The 23 databases available cover business, commerce, science and law. Dun & Bradstreet's Key British Enterprises with a database of 20,000 companies is available on this service.

I P Sharp Associates Limited
132 Buckingham Palace Road, London SW1W 9SA. Telephone: 01-730 4567. Contact IPSA for information on their wide range of databases. These include Financial Times Share Information, Business International Economic Forecasts, UK Central Statistical Office and overseas stock market databases.

Statistics and Market Intelligence Library
1 Victoria Street, London SW1H 0ET. Telephone: 01-215 5444 or 5445; Telex: 8811074 (DTHQ G). This library contains material for research on overseas markets including general statistical compilations, statistics of trade, population, production, distribution, prices, employment, transport, finance, energy and development plans. It also has the principal series of UK economic statistics, current trade and telephone directories for all countries, as well as commercially published market surveys. The library is open to the public and information can be requested by letter, telephone, telex or personally.

Stockbrokers' Research and Information Services
Oxford Centre for Management Studies, Oxford. Telephone: (0865)

735422. This is a useful guide to stockbrokers' information available to non-investor clients.

Warwick Statistics Service
University of Warwick Library, Coventry CV4 7AL. Telephone: (0203) 418938; Telex: 31406. The library has a large statistics collection covering many countries. Use of the library and the enquiry service is available to business and commercial organizations on payment of an annual subscription.

Westminster Central Reference Library
33 St Martins Street, London WC2H 7HP. Telephone: 01-930 3274. This library contains commercial books, HMSO publications from 1947 and EEC publications, and offers many of the services mentioned in this chapter. The library is open to the general public from Monday to Saturday. It will deal with straightforward enquiries but does not offer an in-depth research service.

List 2: Data for Individual Companies

The Company Status Report
Credit Ratings Limited, 51 City Road, London EC1Y 1AY. Telephone: 01-251 6675; Telex: 23678. A company status report is a three-page analysis of a company's performance. The first page contains facts and figures for the company, the second page is devoted to the last two years' financial results and the third page is a company/sector comparison showing individual liquidity, profitability and gearing ratios set against quartiles from the industry sector.

Datacards
ICC Datacard Services, 28–42 Banner Street, London EC1Y 8QE. Telephone: 01-608 0525/6; Telex: 23678. The ICC Datacard Service covers all companies on the ICC database. Each card has a detailed four year comparative analysis of a company's report and accounts. It also contains company details and shows the company's activities, industrial classification and 25 financial ratios. Cards can be ordered on an individual basis and there is an updating service which provides the new datacard for a selected company as soon as it is available.

Dataline
Finsbury Data Services Limited, 68–74 Carter Lane, London EC4. Telephone: 01-248 9828; Telex: 892520. Dataline provides on-line access to a database of 3,000 UK and overseas company accounts from the EXSTAT database. The information is in a standardized, structured format and comprises income statements, balance sheets, financing tables and ratios. Dataline has a financial modelling system which enables forecasts to be derived from projections of key variables. Dataline is used with the Textline terminals.

Datastream
Datastream International Limited, Monmouth House, 58–64 City Road, London EC1Y 2AL. Telephone: 01-250 3000; Telex: 884230. Datastream offers a huge amount of regularly updated data collected from approximately 20,000 equities around the world. Datastream services allow research on market performance, analysis of company accounts and search facilities. Also available are programs covering traded options; Z-scores; market indices; exchange rates; interest rates and commodities; economic series; and key indicators.

Dunsdata Business Information Reports
Dun & Bradstreet Limited, 26–32 Clifton Street, London EC2P 2LY. Telephone: 01-377 4377; Telex: 886697. Dun & Bradstreet's *Business Information Report* offers basic facts about the subject company, its credit rating and payment score, its balance sheet and income statement and some additional financial detail. A brief company history is included as well as notes on the company's aspirations and outlook. Reports can be provided on-line via a terminal, by telex, diskette, telephone, mail or messenger service.

EXSTAT
Extel Statistical Services Limited, 37–45 Paul Street, London EC2A 4PB. Telephone: 01-253 3400; Telex: 262687. EXSTAT is a database of company financial information in computer-readable form. The data comes from the same source as Extel Cards and covers 3,500 industrial and commercial companies both quoted and un-quoted. Each UK company has 319 data items for each of the 14 years covered. EXSTAT is updated every week and is available through several computer bureaux time-sharing services. It can also be sup-plied on standard magnetic tape.

Extel Company Information Card Services United Kingdom

Extel Statistical Services Limited, 37–45 Paul Street, London EC2A 4PB. Telephone: 01-253 3400; Telex: 262687. Extel Cards provide standardized financial data for 3,000 listed UK companies, 2,200 unquoted companies and a large number of overseas companies. Each card shows the profit and loss account, the balance sheet and other information taken from the accounts. There are several different cards and several different services, so ask for the *Extel Card Users' Guide*.

Extel Handbook of Market Leaders

Extel Statistical Services Limited, 37–45 Paul Street, London EC2A 4PB. Telephone: 01-253 3400; Telex: 26287. This is a quick-reference book based on the more detailed Extel Card Service. It covers the 750 companies in the FT Actuaries' Index and for each there is a page of summarized financial information. This includes profit and loss figures, capital employed figures, ordinary share records, activities and future prospects.

ICC Company Information Services

ICC, 51 City Road, London EC1Y 1AY. Telephone: 01-251 4941; Telex: 23578. ICC offers a 24-hour return-of-post service providing copies of company accounts. They also have a full search service which provides current company details and a telephone enquiry service which can instantly tell you the date of the last filed accounts and annual return of any UK company.

ICC American Company Information Service

ICC – American Company Information Services, 51 City Road, London EC1Y 1AY. Telephone: 01-251 4941; Telex: 23678. ICC's American Company Information Service can provide information on public or private companies in the USA.

ICC Databases on Dialog

ICC Database, ICC House, 81 City Road, London EC1Y 1BD. Telephone: 01-250 3922; Telex: 23678. ICC has two on-line databases. The first is a directory of 1,000,000 companies in the UK. The second consists of 12,000 full data sheets and 48,000 abridged data sheets. Full data sheets contain 100 items of financial data for each of four years and about 20 financial ratios. The databases can be used to search for companies and to rank them on various criteria.

ICC European Company Information Service
ICC – European Information Services, 51 City Road, London
EC1Y 1AY. Telephone: 01-251 4942; Telex: 23678. ICC's European
Service provides various reports including accounts, status reports
and annual returns for companies registered in Belgium, Denmark,
France, Germany, Holland, Norway, Sweden, Italy and Finland. ICC
has 1,000 European company accounts on record in London.

Jordan Line Services
Jordan & Sons (Surveys) Limited, Jordan House, Brunswick Place,
London N1 6EE. Telephone: 01-253 3030. This business information
service offers the *Companies' Registry Index and Directory* on-line. In
addition, the Jordan Watch database contains corporate and financial
data on up to 100,000 trading companies. A postal information service
is also available.

McCarthy Cards
McCarthy Information Limited, Manor House, Ash Walk, Warminster,
Wiltshire BA12 8PY. Telephone: (0985) 215151. McCarthy Cards are
information sheets containing all relevant news and comment articles
from the leading international newspapers and financial journals.
The full text of most articles is printed on the cards. Each McCarthy
Card is indexed by company or industry group and shows the date
and source of articles. There are pre-selected services for the following groups of companies: UK Quoted, UK Unquoted, Australian,
European, North American, Industry. The Cards are available in
paper or microfiche form.

McCarthy Company Profile Service
McCarthy Information Limited, Manor House, Ash Walk, Warminister,
Wiltshire BA12 8PY. Telephone: (0985) 215151. Each company profile
consists of a dossier containing one year's McCarthy Cards. The latest
report and accounts and any other published information such as
interim statements or press releases are also included.

McCarthy Information Reports and Accounts Service (MIRAC)
McCarthy Information Limited, Manor House, Ash Walk, Warminister,
Wiltshire BA12 8PY. Telephone: (0985) 215151. Microfiched copies of
company reports and accounts are available within a week of publication and despatched to MIRAC subscribers automatically. A full
service is available which covers 2,800 companies or alternatively a

selective service can be tailored to meet users' needs. One-off copies of the accounts can also be supplied.

MicroEXSTAT
EXTEL Statistical Services Limited, 37–45 Paul Street, London EC2A 4PB. Telephone: 01-253 3400; Telex: 262687 (STATS G). This is a powerful microcomputer-based service which can carry out most of the tasks associated with analysing company accounts. It provides standardized data for over 2,200 UK companies but the data for other companies can easily be entered. Standard analysis reports include balance sheet, income statements, ratios and funds flow statements. Also, reports can be tailored to suit the precise needs of the user. The database can be searched to find companies with particular characteristics and the data can be passed to other software for forecasting purposes.

Research Index
Business Surveys Limited, PO Box 21, Dorking, Surrey RH5 4EE. This is a fortnightly index to articles and news of business interest. One section in the index covers industrial and commercial news and reports and is arranged alphabetically under subject headings. The second section is concerned with articles about particular companies. This is purely an index – there are no abstracts.

Searchline
Extel Statistical Services Limited, 37–45 Paul Street, London EC2A 4PB. Telephone: 01-253 3400 ext. 238; Telex: 262687 (STATSG). Searchline offers company information by post. A full search will provide a company's annual return as well as its report and accounts.

Textline
Finsbury Data Services Limited, 68 Carter Lane, London EC4. Telephone: 01-248 9828; Telex: 892520. Textline is an on-line business text database providing current facts, economic data, trends, forecasts and comment from business publications worldwide. These publications include national newspapers, business journals, press releases, news tapes, corporate financial reports, newsletters etc.

List 3: Industry and Aggregate Company Data

Business Ratio Reports
ICC Limited, 28–42 Banner Street, London EC1Y 8QE. Telephone: 01-253 3906; Telex: 23678. *Business Ratio Reports* consist of data sheets for up to 100 leading companies in each of the industry sectors covered. Information included on the sheets consists of company details, up to four years' financial data and 19 key ratios. Growth-rate statistics for sales, profits, wages, assets, exports and capital employed are included.

ICC Financial Survey and Company Directory
ICC Financial Surveys, 28–42 Banner Street, London EC1Y 8QE. Telephone: 01-253 9736; Telex: 23678. Each survey provides two lists of the companies in an industry sector. The first includes two years' figures for turnover, total assets, current liabilities, profits before tax and payments to directors. The second has marketing data and gives the company's names and addresses as well as their activities and ultimate owners.

Jordans Business Surveys
Jordan & Sons Surveys Limited, Jordan House, Brunswick Place, London N1 6EE. Telephone: 01-253 3030; Telex: 261010. These surveys provide information on business prospects, market trends, financial performance, competitive analysis and business leads. Jordans also provide financial surveys, mainly specializing in data for private companies. For an up-to-date list of the surveys available and information on Jordans business services ask for their *Quarterly Review*.

Key Note Reports
Key Note Publications Limited, 28–42 Banner Street, London EC1Y 8QE. Telephone: 01-253 3006; Telex: 23678. Each report covers a specific industry. It analyses the industry structure, the major manufacturers and brands in the sector, as well as the total market size and shares. There is an overview of recent developments and trends within the market and of future prospects. In addition there is an analysis of the financial state of the market with data abstracted from several major companies, a list of further information to help additional research and a list of recent press articles about the industry sector.

List 4: Market Research Indexes and Abstracts

The A–Z of UK Marketing Information Sources

Euromonitor Publications Limited, 87–8 Turnmill Street, London EC1M 5QU. Telephone: 01-251 8024. This is a very useful paperback book providing a comprehensive guide to the different types and sources of marketing information available.

Financial Times Monthly Index

Financial Times Business Enterprises Limited, Bracken House, 10 Cannon Street, London EC4P 4BY. Telephone: 01-248 8000. This is a monthly index to articles in the *Financial Times*. Articles are indexed under subject headings such as companies, products and people.

Findex, Directory of Market Research Reports, Studies & Surveys

SVP United Kingdom, 12 Argyll Street, London W1V 1AB. Telephone: 01-734 9278. This is an annual international index to market and business research. It contains consumer studies, surveys, syndicated and multi-client studies, subscription report services and published reports on management and business. About 9,000 reports are listed. The UK office offers a full information service on a subscription basis and will carry out specific searches. FINDEX, the database corresponding to this directory, is available on the DIALOG on-line service.

International Directory of Published Market Research

British Overseas Trade Board & Arlington Management Publications, 87 Jermyn Street, London SW1Y 6JD. Telephone: 01-930 3638; Telex: 917835. This directory, which lists over 8,000 market research reports, has an alphabetical subject index and a source index which gives the names and address of publishers. There are references to reports from more than 100 countries.

Market Research Abstracts

Market Research Society, 15 Belgrave Square, London SW1X 8PF. Telephone: 01-235 4709. Besides covering marketing and advertising research, there are abstracts from papers in statistics, psychology and sociology. Regular section headings cover statistical models and forecasting. Two editions are published each year and between them contain about 300 abstracts from UK and American journals and conference papers.

Market Research Reports and Industry Surveys
Science Reference Library (External Relations & Liaison Section), 25 Southampton Buildings, London WC2A 1AW. Telephone: 01-405 8721 ext. 3344/3345; Telex: 266959. This is an index of recent market research reports and industry surveys. It has a subject and a publisher index and covers a wide range of subjects and countries. All the reports listed are available at the Science Reference Library.

Marketing Surveys Index
Marketing Strategies for Industry (UK) Limited, 22 Wates Way, Mitcham, Surrey CR4 4HR. Telephone: 01-640 6621; Telex: 27950 REF 1153. This monthly index contains details of UK current market research reports. It contains a useful list of publishers and their addresses and a supplement listing current academic research in marketing. *Marketing Surveys Index* is published in association with the Institute of Marketing.

Reports Index
Business Surveys Limited, PO Box 21, Dorking, Surrey RH5 4EE. This is a bi-monthly index to reports published by HMSO, other government bodies, industrial and financial companies, research organizations, trade and professional organizations, stockbrokers and the EEC. The items are listed under subject headings; brief abstracts and details on the price and availability of the various reports are printed.

The Top 2000 Directories and Annuals 1984/85
Alan Armstrong and Associates limited, 72–6 Park Road, London NW1 4SH. This is an annual directory giving the names of 2,000 trade directories and reference publications.

List 5: Market Research Sources

EIU Reviews and Quarterlies
The Economist Intelligence Unit, Spencer House, 27 St James's Place, London SW1A 1NT. Telephone: 01-493 6711; Telex: 266353. The Economist Intelligence Unit produces a range of quarterly and monthly publications on energy, industries, multi-national business, products and marketing. Their publications list gives full details.

Larsen Sweeney Publications
Larsen Sweeney Publications Limited, PO Box 70415, 1007 KK,

Amsterdam, Netherlands. Telephone: (020) 73 18 08; Telex: 18778. The Larsen Sweeney reports are taken from a database of European product and market information and are based on original surveys and forecasts. Reports are available in printed form or by access to the databases. The reports cover 16 European countries.

Market Research Great Britain
Euromonitor Publications Limited, 87–8 Turnmill Street, London EC1M 5QU. Telephone: 01-251 8024; Telex: 21120 MONREF G. Each month *Market Research* offers seven market reports chosen mainly from the major consumer markets. The reports contain an assessment of recent trends, information on the value of the market, five-year sales trends, distribution and market penetration. They also provide brand share information and forecasts for the main manufacturers.

Market Forecasts
Market Assessment Publications, 2 Duncan Terrace, London N1 8BZ. Telephone: 01-278 9517. *Market Forecasts* is an annual publication which covers forecasts on 200 UK consumer markets and is aimed at investors and manufacturers considering diversification into other markets.

Market Intelligence
Mintel Publications Limited, KAE House, 7 Arundel Street, London WC2R 3DR. Telephone: 01-836 1814; Telex: 21405 KAEMIN G. Each monthly survey analyses five different consumer markets or services and contains information on market size and trends, imports and exports, manufacturers and brand shares, distribution and promotion.

Planning Consumer Markets
Henley Centre for Forecasting, 2 Tudor Street, Blackfriars, London EC4Y 0AA. Telephone: 01-353 9961; Telex: 298817. *Planning Consumer Markets* is a quarterly journal of economic forecasts for use in market research. Each journal contains forecasts for the short, medium and long term which cover such subjects as income levels, savings flows, consumer spending, population trends and regional analyses.

Retail Business
Economist Intelligence Unit, Spencer House, 27 St James's Place, London SW1A 1NT. Telephone: 01-493 6711; Telex: 266353. *Retail Business* is a monthly journal of UK market information on consumer products. Product reviews cover production, consumption and con-

sumer spending with short-term forecasts for each product sector. Market profiles and company profiles cover all aspects of retailing and retailers.

UK Market Reports
Euromonitor Publications Limited, 87–8 Turnmill Street, London EC1M 5QU. Telephone: 01-251 8024; Telex: 21120 MONREF G. Each year Euromonitor publishes a number of market reports on a wide range of consumer markets. See their publications' list for further details.

List 6: National and International Data Sources

Annual Abstract of Statistics
Published by HMSO for the Central Statistical Office. The *Annual Abstract* has over 360 tables containing 11 years of data which cover most aspects of economic, social and industrial life in the UK.

Business Monitors
HMSO Books, Freepost, Norwich NR3 1BR. Telephone: (0603) 22211; Telex: 97301. These are a series of publications giving business statistics for manufacturing, energy, mining, service and distributive industries. For a complete list of all the *Monitors* and for suggestions on how to use them send for *Business Monitors: what are they and how can they help your business?* from HMSO at Norwich.

CSO Macro-Economic Databank
Operated for CSO by SIA Computer Services, Ebury Gate, 23 Lower Belgrave Street, London SW1W 0NW. Telephone: 01-730 4544. The data stored cover the index of industrial production, national income and expenditure, balance of payments, prices, earnings, employment and financial statistics, cyclical indicators and commodity flow accounts. Data are available on magnetic tape or in computer printout form.

Directory of British Official Publications: A Guide to Sources
Mansell Publishing, 1981. This directory covers data sources from central government, research councils and nationalized industries. There are two indexes, one by subject and the other by organization.

Economic Progress Report
HM Treasury, The Publications Division, Central Office of Information,

Hercules Road, London SE1 7DU. This is a free monthly publication containing the Treasury's current economic assessment.

Economic Trends
Published by HMSO for the Central Statistical Office. *Economic Trends* presents a commentary and a selection of tables and charts which provide a broad background to trends in the UK economy.

Employment Gazette
Published by HMSO for the Department of Employment. This is a monthly journal containing labour market data.

Family Expenditure Survey
Published by HMSO for the Department of Employment. This is an annual survey containing data on household expenditure and income. A guide to the survey, *Family Expenditure Survey: handbook on the sample, fieldwork, coding procedures, and related methodological experiments* is produced by the Social Survey Division of the Office of Population Censuses and Surveys.

Financial Statistics
Published by HMSO for the Central Statistical Office. This is a monthly publication with key financial and monetary statistics.

Financial Times Stats Fiche
McCarthy Information Limited, Manor House, Ash Walk, Warminster, Wiltshire BA12 8PY. Telephone: (0985) 215151. This service supplies two microfiches per week, each containing three days' statistics on unit trust prices, share prices, the FTA indices, daily exchange rates, the world value of the pound and the world value of the dollar.

General Household Survey
Published by HMSO for the Office of Population Censuses & Surveys. This annual survey contains data on population, housing, employment, education and health.

Government Statistics: A Brief Guide to Sources
Central Statistical Office (CSO), Press and Information Service, Room 58/G, Central Statistical Office, Great George Street, London SW1P 3AQ. This excellent free guide contains a description of the Government Statistical Service. There is a publications' list and a list of government departments and the statistics they produce. Depart-

ment telephone numbers for specific enquiries and information on where to buy HMSO and CSO publications are given.

Guide to Official Statistics
Published by HMSO for the Central Statistical Office. The *Guide to Official Statistics* is published twice yearly and covers about 2,500 sources of government data published within the last ten years. The sources are listed by subject and there is a comprehensive index.

HMSO Books: A Guide to Publications and Services
Publicity Department, HMSO Books, St Crispins, Duke Street, Norwich NR3 1PD or Freepost, Norwich NR3 1PD. Telephone: (0603) 22211; Telex: 97301. This is a free guide to HMSO publications and services. It contains full details on how to order directly from HMSO and lists HMSO bookshops and agents. The services referred to in the title are a comprehensive bibliographic and standing order service for HMSO publications.

Housing and Construction Statistics
Published by HMSO for the Department of the Environment. This is an annual publication with data on housing starts and completions.

Monthly Digest of Statistics
Published by HMSO for the Central Statistical Office. The CSO *Monthly Digest of Statistics* is a collection of the main series from all government departments. Tables show quarterly and monthly figures over the last two years as well as annual figures for a longer period.

National Income & Expenditure 'Blue Book'
Published by HMSO for the Central Statistical Office. The 'Blue Book' is an annual publication and provides a data source for everyone concerned with macroeconomic policies and studies. It is the principal publication for national accounts statistics and provides detailed estimates of national income and expenditure for the UK. There is a publication called *The National Accounts – A Short Guide* (Studies in Official Statistics No. 36, August 1981) which explains the structure of the 'Blue Book' and the system of national accounts.

OPCS Monitors
Office of Population Censuses and Surveys, Information Branch (Dept. GS), OPCS, St Catherines House, 10 Kingsway, London WC2B 6JP. Telephone: 01-242 0262. These reports provide the most

recent population estimates and projections as well as migration figures.

Population Trends
Published by HMSO for Office of Population Censuses & Surveys. This is a quarterly journal which contains statistical tables on population.

Regional Trends
Published by HMSO for the Central Statistical Office. This report contains a selection of statistics concerning regional variations in the UK.

Social Trends
Published by HMSO for the Central Statistical Office. This is an annual CSO publication which provides statistical information on social trends in the UK. It covers population, households and families, education, employment, income and wealth, resources and expenditure, health and social services etc.

Statistical News
Published by HMSO for the Central Statistical Office. This is a quarterly journal which covers development in UK official statistics.

Statistics Europe: Sources for Social, Economic & Market Research
CBD Research, 4th Edition 1981. This publication contains the names of organizations which collect and publish statistical material. It also names libraries and the main bibliographies of statistics. There is a list by subject of the statistical publications for each country.

Transport Statistics Great Britain
Published by HMSO for the Department of Transport. Statistics of freight and personal transport are provided in this annual survey.

List 7: Macroeconomic Forecasts

Cambridge Economic Policy Review
Cambridge Economic Policy Group. This is a twice-yearly macro-economic forecast of the UK.

The Director's Guide
Henley Centre for Forecasting, 2 Tudor Street, Blackfriars, London EC4Y 0AA. Telephone: 01-353 9961; Telex: 298817. The macro-economic forecasts in the monthly *Director's Guide* cover a wide variety of topics and are for two years ahead. In each section there are forecasts, commentary and recommended courses of action. In addition each guide has the most recent official statistics on prices, earnings, costs and retail sales.

Economic Forecasts
Phillips & Drew, 120 Moorgate, London EC2M 6XP. Telephone: 01-628 4444; Telex: 291163. Phillips & Drew produce monthly macro-economic forecasts for the UK.

Economic Outlook
London Business School, Sussex Place, Regent's Park, London NW1 4SA. Telephone: 01-262 5050; Telex: 27461. Along with the National Institute Economic Review forecast this is one of the most detailed and most respected of the macroeconomic forecasts that are currently available. *Economic Outlook* is published three times a year and updated monthly.

Economic Situation Report
Confederation of British Industry, Centre Point, 103 New Oxford Street, London WC1A 1DU. Telephone: 01-379 7400. Since 1958 the CBI has conducted highly reliable surveys of recent and expected trends in manufacturing industry. In 1975 it started to publish forecasts of the whole economy partly based on those surveys. The forecasts are published three or four times per year.

EIU Outlooks – Annual Publications
The Economist Intelligence Unit, Spencer House, 27 St James's Place, London SW1A 1NT. Telephone: 01-493 6711; Telex: 266353. EIU *World Outlook* provides separate detailed forecasts of likely trends in the economies of over 160 countries. See the EIU publications' list for full details.

European Trends
The Economist Intelligence Unit, Spencer House, 27 St James's Place, London SW1A 1NT. Telephone: 01-493 6711; Telex: 266353. This forecast covers the developments in the EEC which businessmen and administrators need to know. It includes internal and external political,

legal and economic relations. Besides various reports, each issue contains statistical appendices showing comparative trends in the main economic indicators. An *Annual Reference Supplement* provides basic background data.

Financial Outlook
London Business School, Sussex Place, Regent's Park, London NW1 4SA. Telephone: 01-262 5050; Telex: 27461. This is an economic forecast specializing in the financial markets. It is produced three times per year.

Financial Statement & Budget Report
HM Treasury, The Publications Division, Central Office of Information, Hercules Road, London SE1 7DU. Published twice yearly, this is the official Treasury macroeconomic forecast.

Framework Forecasts for the UK Economy
Henley Centre for Forecasting, 2 Tudor Street, Blackfriars, London EC4Y 0AA. Telephone: 01-353 9961; Telex: 298817. Framework forecasts are monthly macroeconomic forecasts which give both short-term and five-year views of the future. Their projections cover, among other topics, costs and prices, personal incomes, and spending by category of expenditure.

National Institute Economic Review
National Institute for Economic and Social Research, 2 Dean Trench Street, Smith Square, London SW1P 3HE. Telephone: 01-222 7665. NIESR produces a quarterly macroeconomic forecast which is one of the most detailed and respected predictions of the UK economy. About once a year industrial sector forecasts are also included.

OECD Economic Outlook
Organization for Economic Co-operation and Development. Available from HMSO. The *Economic Outlook* is a twice-yearly macroeconomic forecast produced in English. It covers the OECD countries in some detail and also gives UK forecasts.

OECD Economic Surveys: UK
Organization for Economic Co-operation and Development. Available from HMSO. Once a year the OECD produces a macroeconomic forecast for the economy of each of its members. The reports are in English and are remarkably cheap, costing only about £2 per country.

Quarterly Economic Reviews Service
The Economist Intelligence Unit, Spencer House, 27 St James's Place,
London SW1A 1NT. Telephone: 01-253 3400; Telex: 266353. There are
83 reviews covering political, economic and business conditions in
over 160 countries. They provide a business analysis of the latest
economic indicators for the countries covered. Each review contains a
page on economic structure giving GDP (by sector), exports, imports,
balance of payments and foreign debt. Another section reports on
economic prospects for nine key economies. Statistical appendices
give key data and detailed foreign trade figures.

Further Reading

The bibliography suggests some further reading. These books and articles listed are those that a reader might reasonably want to move on to after reading this book. They have been chosen on the grounds either that they fill out and reinforce topics covered or that they are the next stage of development of a topic. Some of them are more technical than this text. The brief description of each of them gives the reader some idea of what to expect. It is not at all an exhaustive list; it is merely those readings that most readers might now feel ready to tackle and want to pursue.

All Chapters

1) J.S. Armstrong, *Long Range Forecasting*, Wiley and Sons, 1978. A long book but do not be put off: it is very readable. It is also perhaps the best book for dealing with all the wider aspects of business forecasting. Armstrong directs attention to the important issues in forecasting. He gently and wittily takes to task those who make forecasting more technical than it might be.
2) R. Fildes, D. Dewes and S. Howell, *A Bibliography of Business and Economic Forecasting*, Gower, 1981. Good for reference purposes. It is likely to be updated from time to time.
3) S. Makridakis and S.C. Wheelwright, *Forecasting: Methods and Applications*, Wiley and Sons, 1978. This is a good reference book covering a wide range of techniques. Mostly the explanations are lucid. It is for the manager with some quantitative ability.
4) S.C. Wheelright and S. Makridakis, *Management and Forecasting*, Wiley and Sons, 1980. Yes, it is the same duo but in a different order. This book is shorter, covering fewer techniques but dealing more with management considerations.

5) *The Journal of Forecasting*, Wiley and Sons, quarterly journal. Many of the articles in this recently introduced (1982) journal are of a technical nature. However, there are others that have a management emphasis and these are usually very worthwhile.

Chapter 1

1) R. Hooke, *How to tell the Liars from the Statisticians*, Dekker, 1983. This book discusses how *conceptual* errors in statistics can and do arise. This is a useful indication of where forecasting errors can arise.
2) G.M. Jenkins, *Practical Experiences in Business Forecasting*, G.M. Jenkins and Partners, 1976. Not all *that* practical. Certainly not very easy to read, unless you are already well-versed in forecasting techniques. But many of the management aspects of forecasting discussed in *The Manager's Guide* . . . are based on Jenkins' work.

Chapter 2

1) R.U. Ayers, *Technological Forecasting and Long Range Planning*, McGraw–Hill, 1969. Becoming dated now but still recognized as a well presented review of qualitative forecasting methods.
2) P.M. Hauser, *Social Statistics in Use*, Russell Sage, 1975. The free speech example is taken from here.
3) T.J. Gordon and H. Hayward, 'Initial Experiment with Cross Impact Matrix Method of Forecasting', *Futures* 1, No. 2, December 1968. The article gives an application of the cross impact technique.

Chapter 3

1) J.E. Freund and F.J. Williams, *Elementary Business Statistics*, Prentice Hall, 4th edition. A most acceptable explanation of the basic concepts of regression and correlation.
2) L.L. Lapin, *Statistics for Modern Managers*, Harcourt and Jovanovich, 1982. Another good explanation of regression and correlation, but covering more ground and including more statistics.

Chapter 4

1) C.D. Lewis, *Industrial and Business Forecasting Methods*, Butterworths, 1982. A devotee of smoothing techniques. Comprehensive coverage

of these techniques especially, as the title implies, in an industrial context.

2) C.R. Nelson, *Applied Time Series Analysis*, Holden–Day, 1973. The Box–Jenkins technique is, according to many surveys, the most accurate of the time series forecasting methods. It is also one of the most technically complicated. Box and Jenkins' own book (*Time Series Analysis*, Holden–Day, 1976) is difficult to understand for non-specialists (and many specialists). Nelson gives one of the most lucid descriptions of the technique, together with practical examples. Even so, the Box–Jenkins technique is not for the faint-hearted.

3) D.W. Trigg and D.H. Leach, 'Exponential Smoothing with an Adaptive Response Rate', *Operational Research Quarterly* Vol. 18, 1967. A weakness of basic smoothing methods is the choice of smoothing constant and its invariability. Trigg and Leach describe their method for monitoring the smoothing constants and signalling the need for changes.

Chapter 5

1) J. Hirshleifer, 'Where we are in the theory of information?', American Economic Review 1973. Excellent though slightly dated survey paper.

2) H. Raiffa, *Decision Analysis*, Addison Wesley, 1968. Strongly recommended as a thorough introduction to decision analysis. The content and exposition are excellent and assume very little knowledge of mathematics.

3) T.H. Wonnacott and R.J. Wonnacott, *Introductory Statistics for Business and Economics*, John Wiley, 1972. Chapters 15 and 18 of this popular text book contain a good explanation of Bayes' Theorem and its role in statistics. The application to continuous variables is particularly well explained.

Chapter 6

1) J.S. Armstrong, 'Forecasting by extrapolation: Conclusions from 25 years of research', *Interfaces* 14 November/December 1984, 52–66. This very readable study, which is mentioned elsewhere in this book, reviews 39 academic papers which have used time series forecasting methods. Its simple but controversial conclusion is that often sophisticated methods have little advantage over simple methods.

2) S. Makridakis, *et al*, 'The accuracy of extrapolation (time series) methods: Results of a forecasting competition', *Journal of Forecasting*, 1, 1979, 111–53. This important paper, often known as the M-competition, examined the accuracy of naive and sophisticated forecasts for 1001 time series. The results are broadly consistent with Armstrong (1984) above, however a flourishing literature is still investigating the question.

3) P. Newbold and C.W.J. Granger, 'Experience with forecasting univariate time series and the combination of forecasts', *Journal of the Royal Statistical Society*, Series A 137, 1974, 131–65. Chapter 7 compared a number of alternative forecasts but did not attempt to combine them into a 'super forecast'. This paper demonstrates how significant improvements can often be achieved by combining several forecasts.

4) V. Zarnowitz, 'An analysis of annual and multiperiod quarterly forecasts of aggregate income, output and the price level', *Journal of Business*, 52, 1979, 1–33. This paper reviews the accuracy of a number of econometric forecasts for the US economy.

Chapter 7

1) P.J. Harrison and C.F. Stevens, 'A Bayesian Approach to Short-term Forecasting', *Operational Research Quarterly* Vol. 22, No. 4, 1971. The origin of an interesting idea for introducing judgement into a smoothing approach to forecasting. Unfortunately the article is not as clearly written as it might be.

2) R.L. Schultz, 'The implementation of Forecasting Models', *Journal of Forecasting* Vol. 3, No. 1, January–March 1984. A review of research into implementation problems.

Chapter 8

1) K.N. Bhaskar and R.J.W. Housdon, *Accounting, information systems and data processing*, Heinemann, 1985. Part 4 of this recent text book contains a series of short chapters which review different applications of computers in modern management practice. The chapter on corporate modelling (pp. 321–47) is particularly useful.

2) T. Cain and N.W. Cain, *Lotus 1–2–3 at work*, Reston Publishing, 1984. This book provides an excellent and thorough introduction to the Lotus 1–2–3 spreadsheet program. It is not specifically about forecasting but contains plenty of relevant business examples.

3) N. Seitz, *Business forecasting on your personal computer*, Reston Publishing, 1984. As the title suggests this book is about forecasting on a personal computer. It explains how to use a microcomputer to apply most of the standard forecasting techniques. It does not use spreadsheet software but in many cases provides appropriate BASIC programs.

4) D. Shaffer, *Lotus 1–2–3 revealed*, Reston Publishing, 1984. This is another good Lotus 1–2–3 book. It is more advanced than Cain and Cain and concentrates on the powerful features that too many users ignore.

Index